A CELTIC CANVAS

A CELTIC CANVAS

THE LIFE, WORK AND TIMES

of

CAREY MORRIS ARTIST

1882–1968

Glyn Rhys

y Lolfa

First impression 2013

Cover design: Y Lolfa

ISBN: 978-1-84771-6682

Printed and published and bound in Wales by Y Lolfa Cyf.,
Talybont, Ceredigion SY24 5HE.
e-mail ylolfa@ylolfa.com
website www.ylolfa.com
phone (01970) 832 304
fax 832 782

Also by Glyn Rhys
Were Those the Days?
Lost Head in Cors Caron

This book is published with the financial support of the Carmarthenshire Antiquarian Society

I
gofio
am
Carey

This is the first serious consideration of an important body of work. Glyn conducts us past the canvases of artisans and squirearchy, through excerpts from Carey Morris's papers, and into the life of a forgotten Wales immediately prior to World War I. The result is a beautifully illustrated and researched book which is also immensely readable. A book to enjoy.

Elan Closs Stephens

(Professor Emeritus, Aberystwyth University)

A well documented, well illustrated and affectionate portrayal of an accomplished artist by an author who was personally acquainted with his subject. This book will do much to place Carey Morris firmly in the pantheon of Welsh artists, and with its wealth of background detail it will attract a wider readership.

Eiluned Rees

(Local Historian, Carmarthenshire)

This lavishly illustrated book is a considerable contribution to bringing an undervalued artist to the attention of an art loving public. The author's personal knowledge and connections make it essential reading for understanding the creative life and work of the talented artist Carey Morris.

Donald M. Treharne

(Chairman of the Friends of the Glynn Vivian Art Gallery, Swansea)

This beautifully illustrated book gives the reader an insight into the life and times of Llandeilo-born artist Carey Morris. At last a book that will introduce the work of artist Carey Morris to a wider audience. The author's friendship has led him to produce a book of great warmth and insight.

Ann Dorsett

(Curator, Carmarthenshire County Museum & Art Gallery)

IN MEMORIAM CAREY MORRIS (1882–1968)

In the clutter of his studio
he made what I took to be trench tea,
leaves in the cup, hot water. No, Tommy
knew no such luxury, oh no...
But those leaves about my gums and teeth
made me gag as if a whiff of gas still
lingered on the air he breathed, enough to kill
a green recruit like me, or hasten death.

But death spared him then. He was a fighter,
this South Wales Borderer of the Slade
and Newlyn schools, a wheezy raconteur,
who told how Edward Thomas would call by,
sit where I sat, with that 'doomed look' he had,
as if already claimed for history.

Andrew McNeillie

CONTENTS

FOREWORD

It is a real privilege to be given the opportunity to evaluate the work of Carey Morris who, in the opinion of Sir Kyffin Williams, was 'a very talented professional artist'. This privilege has been made possible by this splendid book by Dr Glyn Rhys, a distinguished medical man who has applied his diagnostic talents to examine the life, work and times of Morris. The author has the advantage of having known Carey Morris, of knowing his associations and the heartbeat of his 'beloved Llandeilo'. He traces Carey's background, education, training, and war experience in Belgium and France, together with his life and work as an artist. The book allows us to 'know' Carey Morris, his work, his opinions, his wide-ranging interests, his love of Wales. It allows us to glimpse the mind that shaped his art and the fingers that played the cello. Dr Rhys' observations enhance and elucidate the paintings, and the valuable excerpts from Carey's own recollections are so telling. The informed glosses from Carey Morris and Glyn Rhys are also thought-provoking: the comments on abstract painting and 'modern' sculpture are interesting examples.

Added to Glyn Rhys' splendid, informed work is the invaluable reproduction of paintings, drawings and interesting associations. For many they will be a new, maybe first, acquaintance with Carey's work. For me, Carey Morris has assumed a new significance. I am deeply indebted to Dr Glyn Rhys' diagnostic skills

R. Brinley Jones

ACKNOWLEDGEMENTS

In writing this book, I have done my best to trace and resolve copyright matters and tender my sincere apologies for any oversights. I have drawn upon the knowledge and goodwill of many people and I am exceedingly grateful to all who have proffered advice, and I wish to point out that any errors are mine.

Dr Carey Morris, the great-nephew of the artist, has been of inestimable help with his ready and valuable advice. Dr Brinley Jones, for many years the Director of the University of Wales Press, kindly read my original manuscript, and I offer him my sincere thanks for his continued interest and sound and informed counsel. Professor Andrew McNeillie's poem, 'In Memoriam Carey Morris', paints a vivid and evocative picture of the artist and I am delighted to have had his permission to print it at the beginning of my book.

My especial thanks go to Miles Wynn Cato, the Rt. Hon. Lord Dynevor, Elaine Howells, Wynne Melville Jones, Thomas Lloyd, Peter Lord and William Wilkins.

I am indebted to my Llandeilo, Carmarthenshire and Glamorgan contacts: Elizabeth Clee, Desmond Davies, Margaret Davies, Elinor Jones, Ieuan Jones, Julian Jones, Ieuan Lewis, John Owen, Eiluned Rees and Dr Donald Williams.

I offer my thanks to my Cornish contacts: Janet Barnicoat, Iris Green, Peter Hereward Tresidder and Harold Wearn.

To my links abroad I extend my gratitude: John Gallimore and Morraine Hogbin of New South Wales, Australia and Mary Balsdon of Ontario, Canada.

I remember those who encouraged me, but sadly are no longer with us: the 9th Lord Dynevor, Peter Jenkins, Eirwen Jones, the Rev. Vaughan Morris, Sir Kyffin Williams, Merfyn and Violet Williams.

I wish to convey my thanks to Ann Dorsett of the Carmarthenshire County Museum, Lona Mason of the National Library of Wales, and Ellie Dawkins of the Glynn Vivian Art Gallery. The National Museum of Wales, Cardiff and the Royal Academy of Arts, London were helpful as well. I would also like to acknowledge the interest shown and the help received from the Rev. Towyn Jones, Roy Davies and John Saunders of the Carmarthenshire Antiquarian Society, Keith Rees of the National Wool Museum of Wales, the Honourable Society of Cymmrodorion and the Regimental Museum of the Royal Welsh.

The only pictutes not in private ownership are the portrait of Sir Lewis Morris, which is in the Carmarthenshire County Museum, and the portraits of Judge Johnes, Sir Joseph Bradney, Rutland Boughton, and Sir Vincent Evans, which are in the National Library of Wales: I have permission to include them in the book.

I also thank Heulwen Bulman for her tireless deciphering of my manuscript.

I wish to place on record my gratitude to my publishers Y Lolfa, for their unfailing courtesy and expert guidance in the preparation of this book.

I record my sincere thanks to my daughter Ffion for photographing many of the paintings and drawings, and especially for her meticulous work in scanning and editing all the images.

I am much indebted to my daughter Ceril for composing the couplets which end the final chapter.

Finally, I give my heartfelt thanks to my wife Ann who read the manuscript and suggested the title of the book as well as the chapter headings. Her wise advice has been invaluable throughout.

Glyn Rhys
July 2013

INTRODUCTION

I trust that the title makes it clear that this is a book about the life and times of Carey Morris as much as it is about his work as an artist. Any opinions expressed were informed and framed during my discussions with the artist himself. Much of this book may be viewed as social history which I believe had a profound influence on the work of Carey Morris as an artist.

I was fortunate to have been a friend of Carey Morris during his latter years – a friendship I still cherish.

Where appropriate I have quoted Carey Morris verbatim. During our long and far-ranging discussions, frequently lasting into the early hours, the subject of our interlinked genealogies would inevitably crop up and, to a limited extent, this is reflected in the text. I wish to emphasize that I am not an art critic but, like most people, I am able to describe what I see.

My aim has been to bring Carey Morris into being again, in the hope that the time has now come for his work to be evaluated as was suggested by Sir Kyffin Williams RA in 1977:

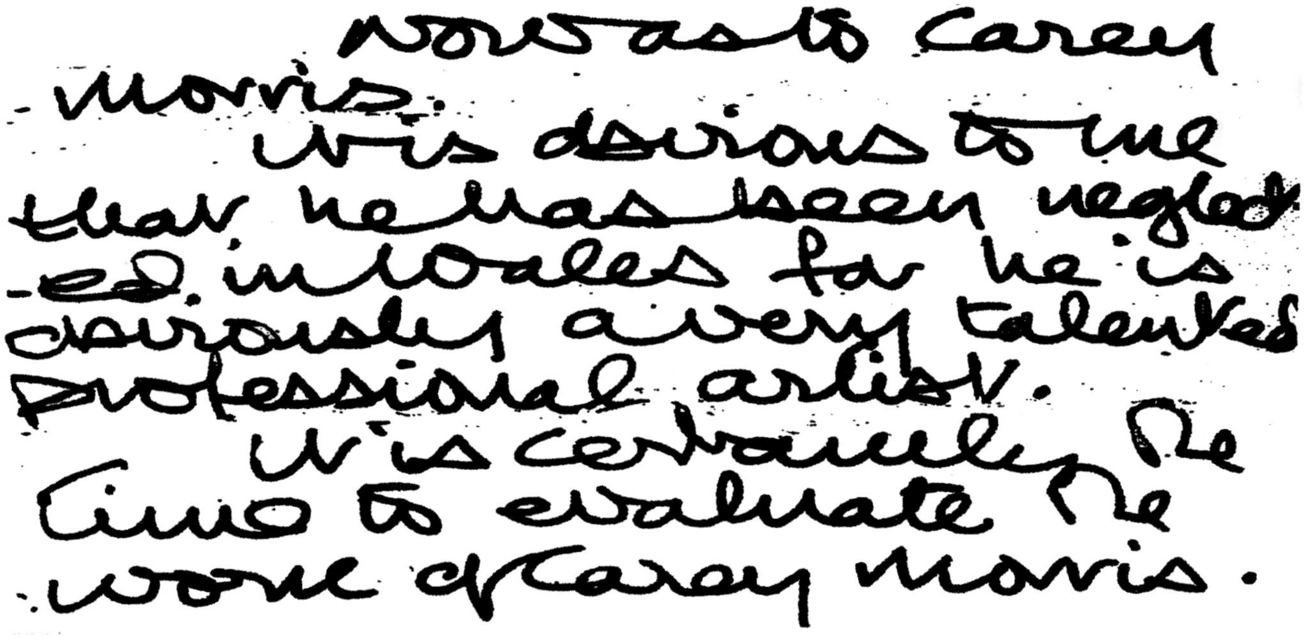
Now as to Carey Morris. It is obvious to me that he has been neglected in Wales for he is obviously a very talented professional artist. It is certainly the time to evaluate the work of Carey Morris.

1 ASPIRATIONS

Carey Morris was born in 1882 in his parents' house near the Castle Hotel opposite London House, Llandeilo, Carmarthenshire. A few years later the family moved to Prospect House, No. 5, Prospect Place, later called 38 Rhosmaen Street. Carey's parents were Benjamin and *Elizabeth* Morris. Carey was the fifth of seven children, five boys and two girls. Two died in infancy, two became vicars, one carried on the family painting and decorating business, while the surviving sister was in charge of the household after the mother's death.

In 1942 Carey Morris began writing an autobiography, but unfortunately the account became fragmented and scattered. Diligent local enquiries and wide-ranging searches, including researches at the National Library of Wales, the University Library at Cambridge and the British Library have yielded nothing of relevance. However I have before me the pages of autobiography that remain, together with a few of his personal papers and some newspaper cuttings. This is how he begins his handwritten autobiography:

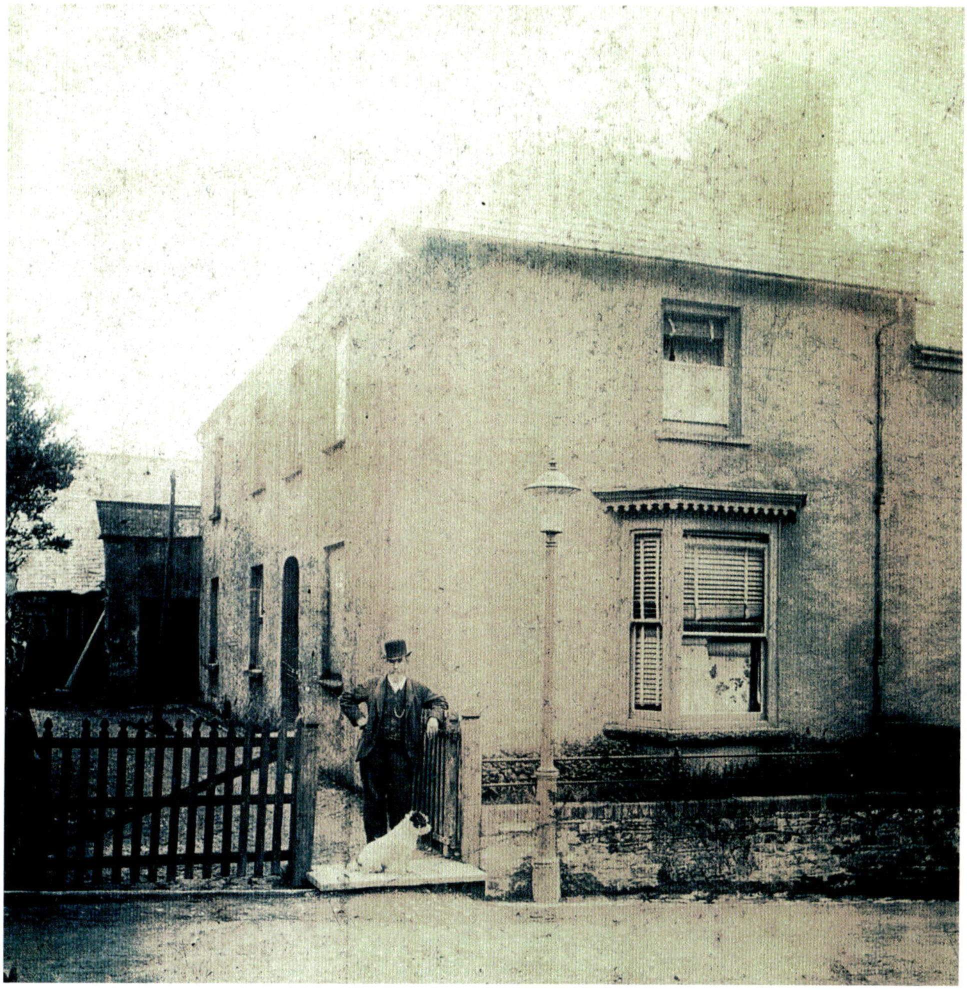

Carey's father outside Prospect House, Llandeilo

Some years before the Great War (1914–18), my sister and I sitting comfortably before a warm fire on a winter's night often passed the time away trying to recall the first incident that we could remember in our childhood. During the heavy bombardments on the Ypres Salient, when life seemed very uncertain, the whole of one's career from childhood passed before one like a cinematograph film. The first incident that I can recall during those periods repeated itself on every occasion during the terrible bombardments. So I start my story, beginning with that incident which I remembered so vividly on those occasions.

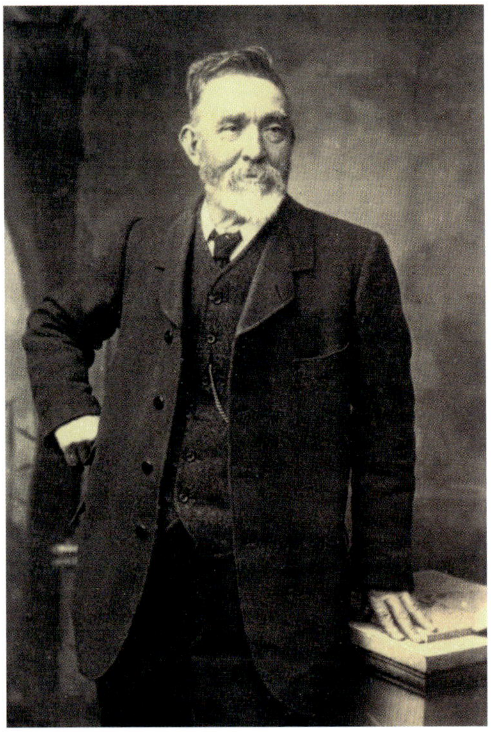

Benjamin Morris

I was a child in my mother's arms and could not possibly be more than two years of age. My father's business partner was an ardent volunteer and was a member of the local volunteer corps. He was on his way to a weekly drill and had turned in to see my father, and also that I should see him in his red tunic and Glengarry cap. Instantly my eyes were fixed on that Glengarry cap, and when the wearer came near enough, I made a quick grab at the headgear and triumphantly placed it on my head.

All was well for the time being but, when it was time for the volunteer to depart to attend the drill, nothing could induce me to part with the fascinating Glengarry cap. Eventually the cap was removed from my head by force and instantly I yelled the roof off at being deprived of the cap. My father, who was most indulgent towards his children, sent my eldest brother to a draper's shop to purchase a cap as near as possible to the Glengarry.

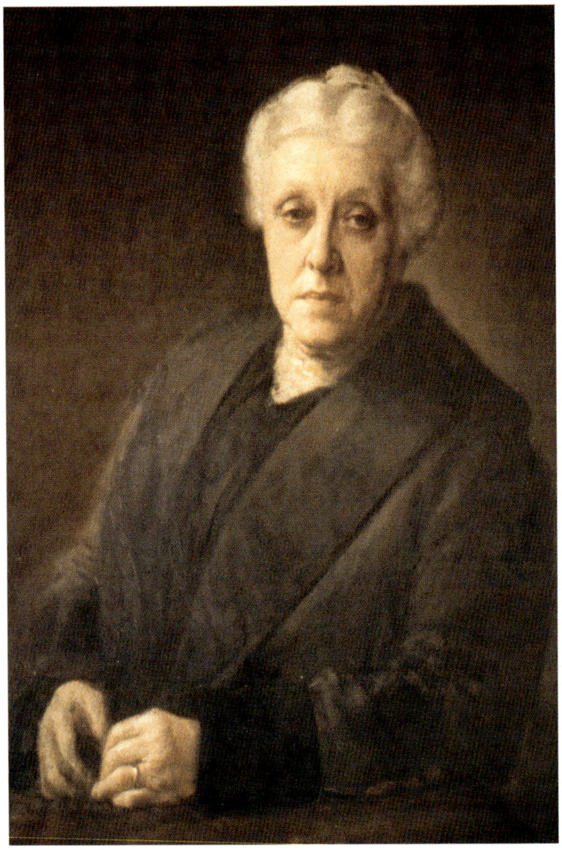

Elizabeth Morris c.1935 30" x 24"

My brother returned with a cap which was, under the circumstances, quite a good substitute but it was a Bonnet – not a Glengarry. At that early age I possessed some degree of astuteness to recognize the difference. I noted that the Bonnet was made of ordinary dark blue cloth, whereas the Glengarry material was of box cloth. Then there was a difference in the braiding. The Glengarry had valuable silk, but the Bonnet had ordinary black braid. The red tassel on top was also different. One was deep vermilion and the other was cheap orange red. The bonnet was placed on my head with some triumph but I would have none of it and removed it off my head and flung it away from me with another outburst of tears. I was indignant and felt I had been deceived.

So Carey's very first memory concerns his appreciation of colours and textures. This, then, is the simple memory which recurred repeatedly, especially during his horrifying experiences during World War I in the trenches at Ypres, under heavy bombardment, when the angel of death was hovering low.

Just like most youngsters Carey always wanted something he couldn't have, as he relates: 'About this time my parents went to Swansea for the day and, passing a well-known shop, I saw a tricycle horse hanging above the doorway. I implored my mother to purchase it for me, but the cost of the article was prohibitive and I was taken away quickly out of sight of the shop.' This shop was probably the department store known as David Evans, demolished by German bombs in World War II.

In the mid 1880s Carey had his photograph taken by G.B. Bradshaw, the Llandeilo photographer, and a few years later, Carey's eldest brother, Robert, started attending art evening classes locally. Carey used to watch him painting, and many years later was to record a similar episode on canvas in an oil entitled *The Old Studio – Robert* which was located at the back of Prospect House, while Carey's own studio was at the front. Even as a child Carey had become, 'quite fascinated with the brushes and tubes of paint', and was 'pestered by boys and grown-ups to draw Red Indians for them'.

Carey attended primary school at Llandeilo National Church School. He remembered teachers seizing the wooden-framed writing slate of any recalcitrant pupil and bringing it down on the boy's head, sometimes with such force that the boy's head broke the slate. The school was opposite the market building at the top of the town (it is now used as a crèche). Carey later attended Llandeilo Institute which was situated near the premises where my great-great-grandfather John Parry had set up his son Edmund as a jeweller and watchmaker in Neuadd Aur, Rhosmaen Street. Carey told me that his father Benjamin remembered Edmund's father John (also a watchmaker, born in 1785) arriving on horseback from Lampeter to visit his son in Llandeilo. Carey recalled that, as an 11-year-old boy, he saw his father tying a black tie in order to attend Edmund's funeral in Llandeilo in 1893. Carey was intrigued that, of the two long-case clocks on permanent display in St Fagan's Castle at the Museum of Welsh Life, one is by the father of all clockmakers, Thomas Tompion *c.*1700, and the other is by my great-great-great-grandfather the renowned Carmarthenshire horologist David Parry, and dated 1775. David Parry had been apprenticed on 16 April 1762 to John Joyce, the master clockmaker of Carmarthen for £50 (equivalent in today's money to £6,900 using the retail price index, or £72,500 using average earnings index).

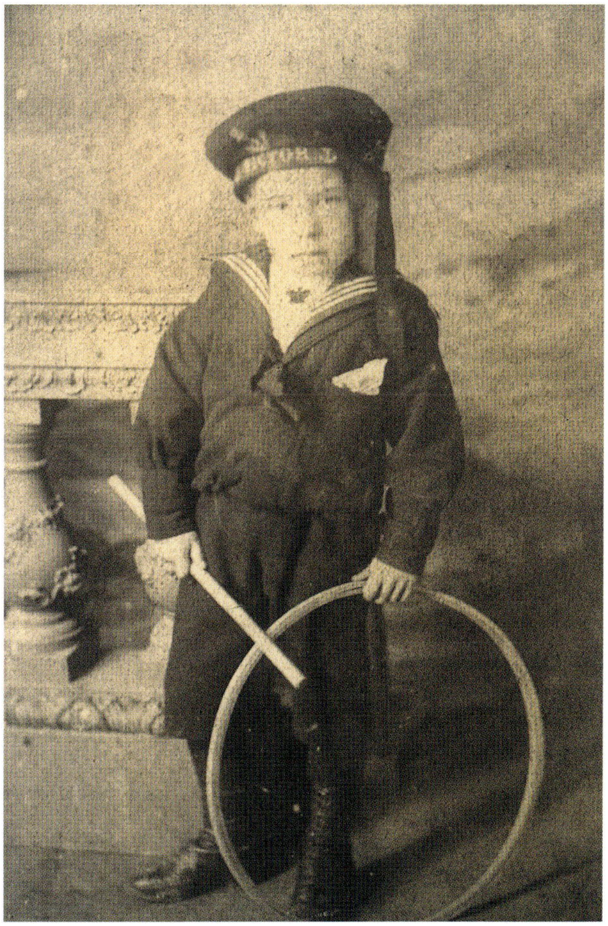

Carey with hoop, photograph taken by G.B. Bradshaw

Edmund's establishment in Rhosmaen Street was opposite the present Cawdor Hotel. Incidentally, it was Lord Cawdor who, at a meeting convened to discuss setting up a grammar school, opposed it saying, "You'll have to find £1,000 first," whereupon 'Davies the Walk' (the Rev. William Davies) the Congregational minister and public benefactor, said, "I have the cheque in my pocket – a gift from Jenkin Jones, Tanyard to buy the land as the site for the school."

Carey was proud of the fact that his name was third on the first register of Llandeilo County Intermediate School, which opened in temporary accommodation in October 1894 when he was 12 years of age. The school was opened officially in a permanent building in 1896 and later became Llandeilo Grammar School. Those were the days when the legendary schoolboy belief that, by placing three hairs strategically across the palm of one's hand, the painful sting of the cane wielded by a teacher could be alleviated. Like the other boys, Carey accepted this as a normal part of school life but, when he was eventually sent to the headmaster for persistently drawing from life in art classes instead of just

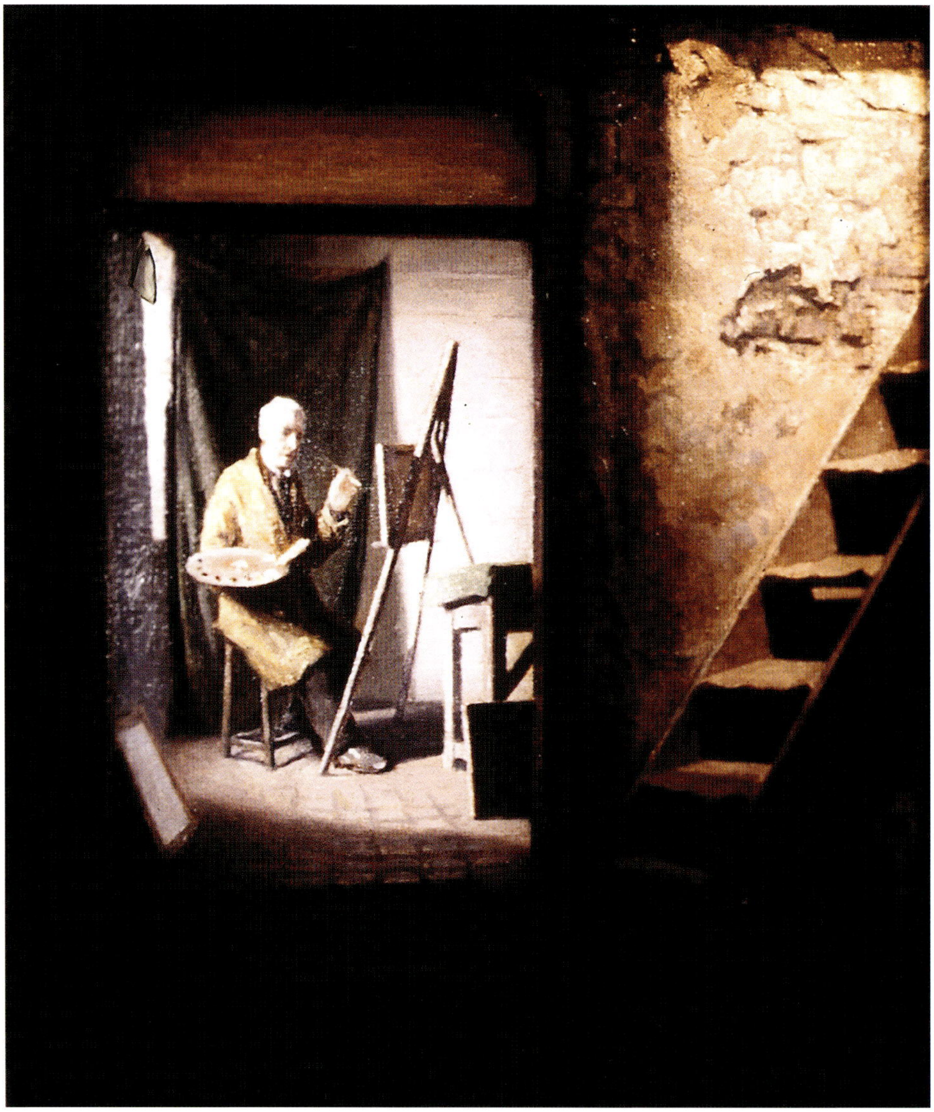

*The Old Studio – Robert c.*1905 18" x 16"

joining up dots as instructed, he was so severely thrashed by that eminent gentleman that his father withdrew him from school and had him privately tutored. The year was 1897 and Carey was 15 years old. Years later Carey commented that it was unbelievable that this system of teaching art existed, as it stifled any talent for art a child might have – a view he reiterated forcibly in his address to the Honourable Society of Cymmrodorion in 1924.

Most of us reminisce about our carefree childhoods and Carey was no exception. He recalls that in his boyhood he spent many happy hours in the Llandeilo Drill Hall listening to the band of the local company of the 1st Volunteer Band of the Welsh Regiment and he writes:

> The children of the town looked forward to the midweek parade when the company, nearly a hundred strong, paraded in uniform (scarlet tunics). Headed by the band, the company marched up to Dynevor Park (by permission of Lord Dynevor) to carry out company drill. When I visited the Tattoo at the Wembley exhibition [and] I watched the pretty little girl dancing at the head of the massed bands, my thoughts went back to those parades at Dynevor Park. The little girls of Llandilo [sic], carried away by the music, danced in their own way at the head of the Volunteer band as it marched up to the park. On Christmas Eve the band played in the streets. I recall those nights as a small boy, lying awake, listening to the playing of Welsh & English Hymn-tunes, also some well-known Welsh airs. They played so softly and with such feeling that I still think of those nights.

Writing of the church parade he says: 'It was the day of the year and the opening of the Season in Llandilo. The tailors and dressmakers had a strenuous time as most boys and girls wore new suits and new frocks for the occasion. This annual fashionable event with its little pageantry has faded away leaving behind happy memories for those who were young at that time.'

Carey's happy memories of the long, hot summer days he spent as a boy in Llandeilo during the last quarter of the nineteenth century make evocative reading: 'My boyhood was full of fun and happiness. I was born in an agricultural town overlooking the lovely vale of

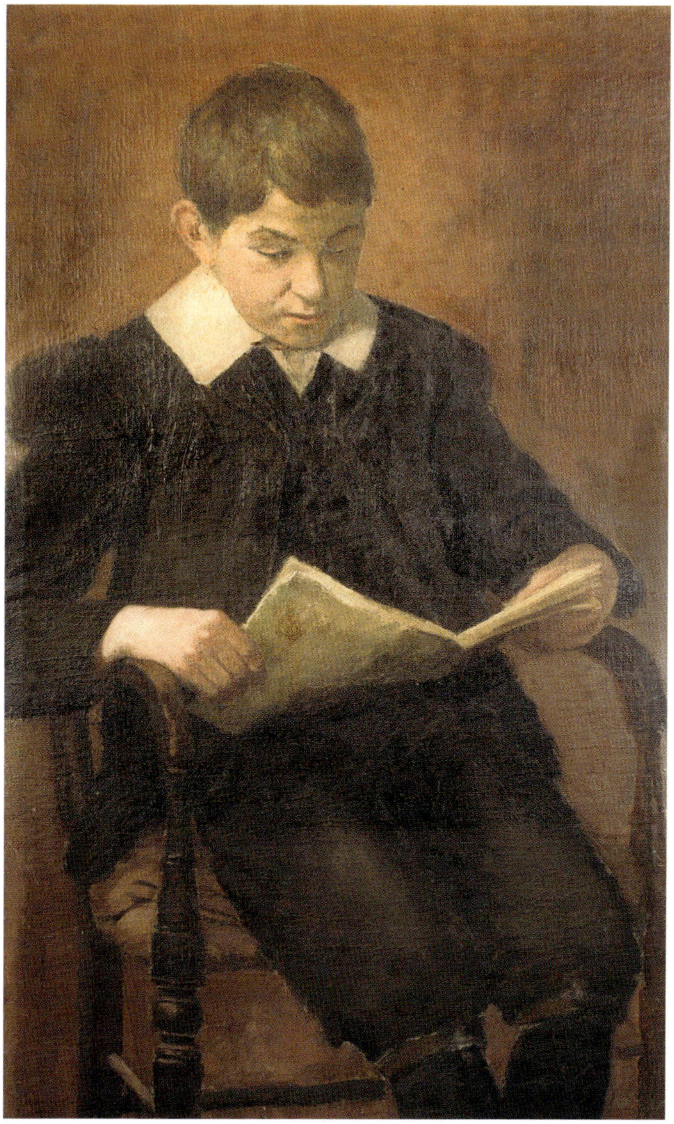

Vaughan Morris 1904 39½" x 22½"

Tywi and in those days there was plenty of good fishing. At an early age I did much fishing, mostly with the artificial fly. I never used worm as a bait. I could not look at the worm being fixed on the hook as the process pained me very much, so I remained a devotee to the artificial fly.'

Maybe this simple statement is an indication of Carey's innate abhorrence of cruelty in any form, even as a young schoolboy. He continues:

> The joy of being on the riverside was too overpowering. I am afraid that in those days I spent too much time fishing. I really should have been at my lessons, but then most of the boys spent their time on the riverside, bathing and fishing. When the autumn arrived there was plenty of fun picking blackberries and nuts. Mushrooms were plentiful in those days. All the usual games came along in their seasons – marbles, hoops, football, hockey, skating and other games. When the winter descended upon us we had long spells of heavy frost, to the delight of all the youngsters of town. There were lovely slides almost on every street, but our fun on those slides was not long lived; the local police were soon on our track but we managed to clear off to another street where there was another slide. The streets in town were mostly hilly and it was exhilarating travelling down the hill on a glassy slide. The boys of today dare not do what we did in those days. It would not be allowed on any condition.

Carey wrote of the recreations pursued by schoolboys in those days. For instance: 'During the summer holidays a group of boys would organise a paper-chase to that romantic spot – Carreg Cennen Castle. On another occasion they would arrange a hike (trundling their iron hoops, large and small) to visit the waterfall at Pontprenaraeth.'

In a nostalgic piece of writing entitled 'The Waterfall', Carey reminisces more about his visit to the Pontprenaraeth waterfall, which is about three miles north-east of Llandeilo:

> I shall never forget my first visit, as a small boy, to the Pontpren waterfall. It was a fine summer day and the sun was shining gloriously. When I entered the dingle, after coming out of the bright sunlight, the place seemed dark, but when I reached the edge of the brook and looked around I was enchanted with my surroundings. To me it seemed as if a fairy with her magic wand had turned the dingle into a fairyland – the home of the little folk 'Tylwyth Teg' – and it would not have surprised me, at my age then, had I seen them running about between the trees. As I looked down on the silent pools, here and there I could see small trout darting hither and thither, disturbed by my intrusion. Treading my way carefully with my companions, between the boulders, I could hear the roar of the waterfall in the near distance. I soon reached a clearing in the dingle, and there before me was the waterfall, a volume of water rushing over a rocky ledge tumbling down into a lower bed of the brook – a fall of about 25 feet. The Araeth, like many brooks from the hills, can be a raging torrent when in spate. When it is in heavy flood the vapour rising from the waterfall can be seen plainly some distance away above the tree-tops of the dingle. Twenty or more years ago a small boy returned with his parents from Canada to Llandilo, where they were staying for a short while. On his return to Llandilo his mother, with a smile, asked him, 'What do you think of Pontpren Falls after seeing Niagara?' Without a smile on his face and in all seriousness the boy replied, 'It is not to be laughed at'.

Carey also wrote that: 'The schoolboys of the mid twentieth century are too sophisticated to indulge in the simple, but healthy, recreations of my boyhood.' How much truer is that of today's schoolboys with all the vast array of electronic gadgetry available to them. Maybe the schoolchildren of the end of the twenty-first century will look back with sympathetic amusement at the 'simple pastimes' of our own schoolchildren of today.

Carey continues: 'A few years ago, after a lapse of many years, I revisited Pontprenaraeth. This time my objective was the little Baptist chapel and not the waterfall. My forebears had attended the services at Bethel Baptist Chapel, Pontprenaraeth, over 100 years ago. My great-grandfather was a minster at this chapel.'

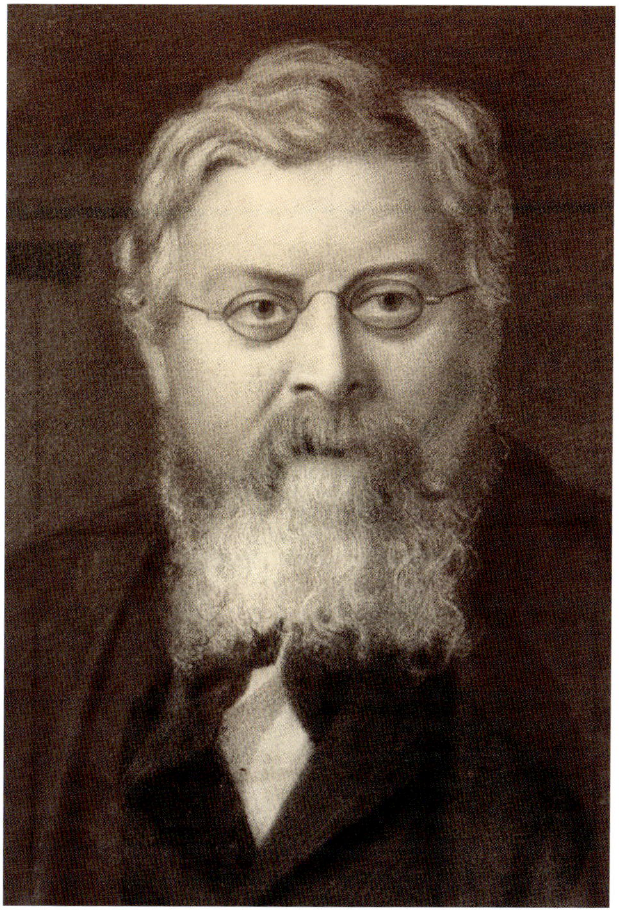

Edmund Parry

Carey's great-grandfather was the Rev. Theophilus Morris whose father was Thomas Morris, a miller and a contractor of mills. He settled with his wife Anne, who hailed from north Wales, in Felin y Pentre, Pontprenaraeth in the latter half of the eighteenth century. Thomas Morris and his wife had many children and three of them became Baptist ministers, including Carey's great-grandfather Theophilus, who remained in Pontprenaraeth as minister in Bethel Chapel – he had a nephew, the Rev. David Morris, who was also a Baptist minister. The ministerial tradition surfaced again in Carey's generation as two of his brothers, Maurice and Vaughan, became vicars. Carey was later to paint *Vaughan* after starting his studies at Newlyn. Vaughan was in his early teens at the time and Carey eight years his senior. This painting shows a studious-looking schoolboy in the dress of the early twentieth century.

As a child Carey remembered that on Sundays his father would bring back many of his friends after morning chapel for discussions on religion and politics, and he recalled that, on some occasions, the arguments became so heated that no one paid any attention to Mrs Morris when she announced lunch was ready. Though she was a domineering woman, it was Carey's father who was obliged to pick up the poker from the fireplace and wave it around shouting, 'Clear the decks, Out! Out! Out!' so that the Morris family could sit down to Sunday lunch after chapel.

During his schooldays, photography became popular, and Carey persuaded his father to buy him a pin-hole camera for 10/– (50p) but, after he had been withdrawn from school, his father bought him a camera with a lens, and he had a lot of fun taking photographs. He reminisced: 'This developed into a stronger urge to do something on a higher artistic plane and draw and paint from life. My thoughts were full of real art and photography had ceased to satisfy me. Then came the avalanche upon me. I must draw and paint portraits from life.'

As Lord Snowdon, the royal photographer, said in 2000 referring to his retrospective exhibition of photography at the National Portrait Gallery, London: 'A photograph is not art – it is a snap. To use the term "portrait" to describe a photograph is pompous – a portrait is something in oils.' Carey's similar sentiments were also echoed by Cornell Capa, the internationally renowned photographer, founding director of the prestigious International Centre of Photography in New York in 1974, who did not regard photography as an art saying, 'The camera is a tool, not a painter's brush'.

When Carey was in his teens he acquired an old copy of *Gray's Anatomy*, the anatomists' bible and, as a result of studying this, he gained a detailed knowledge of surface anatomy as reflected by underlying muscle and bone structure. He also devoured all the books he could find on Rembrandt, Velázquez, Frans Hals and, of course, the greatest of them all, Leonardo da Vinci. In his late teens he worked to a self-imposed timetable and was always wide awake before the time he had set on his alarm clock, impatient for the morning light. He would work on his drawings, taking only midday and tea breaks, and would work by candlelight until eleven at night. In the mid 1890s, Dorofield Hardy, a London artist who had been commissioned to paint copies of some portraits of Lord Dynevor's family, was staying opposite Carey's house at the Imperial Hotel in Llandeilo. Hardy was a well-known copyist of portraits, notably Queen Victoria, Charles I and Clive of India. He became friendly with Carey's father and, as a result, was kind enough to take an interest in Carey's artistic efforts and gave him many art lessons. When Hardy returned to London he asked Carey to send him all his drawings, which he returned with constructive criticisms. This went on for some years, so Carey's teenage work must have made a favourable impression on the artist.

Carey also learnt by watching his brother Robert painting, and he also had lessons from Dyer Davies, who was one of two promising pupils in the same art class as Robert. The other pupil was Lloyd, who came from a well-heeled family, and Dyer Davies, from a poor family. Carey told me that Lloyd was sent to the Slade but did not work hard enough and gave up. Davies was sponsored by Lord Dynevor and others, who paid to send him to art school in Antwerp. On his return to Llandeilo, Davies added the name 'Dyer' in memory of John Dyer, the artist and poet of Aberglasne. Carey much admired Dyer Davies' work – such as the stump drawing Dyer made of my great-great-uncle *Edmund Parry*. After Carey was withdrawn from school, Dyer Davies gave him art lessons at 2/6d. (12½p) per lesson.

Throughout his teens Carey was uncompromisingly assiduous in his dedication to the study of art and the pursuit of his dream of becoming an artist. In Carey's own words: 'Art is a hard taskmaster and success can only be attained by hard work and long hours.'

For relaxation, Carey took to the cello just as another Welsh artist, John Elwyn (1916–97), took to the violin many years later. Carey became so proficient that he was invited to play in the local choral society orchestra by Col. Lloyd Harris, a violinist who played in an orchestra with Sir Edward Elgar. Carey was by now 20 years old, but did not accept this invitation because he was on the point of realizing his dearly-held ambition to go to art school, as he felt he could make no further progress by private study.

He writes:

> My mind wandered far afield and I had visions and ambitions for something quite different. I heard a great deal of the famous Slade School and of Antwerp. The Newlyn School was also much in evidence. I quietly made plans for the future with a view to becoming a pupil at one of these art schools. Neither the Royal Academy School nor the Royal College of Art appealed to me because, at that period, both schools were regarded as being too academic and old-fashioned. The work of the Cornish artists appealed to me very much. Of course I had only seen reproductions of their work. Stanhope A. Forbes, H.S. Tuke, Frank G. Bramley, Mrs Stanhope Forbes, Chevalier Tayler, T.C. Gotch and Walter Langley were the bright stars of the Cornish School at that period. I plumped for Newlyn and wrote to Stanhope Forbes for particulars of his school.

Carey then sent off specimens of his work, and continues: 'I was very excited when I received a letter from a real artist. It was settled that I should proceed to Newlyn in the first week of October. This was in the year 1902.'

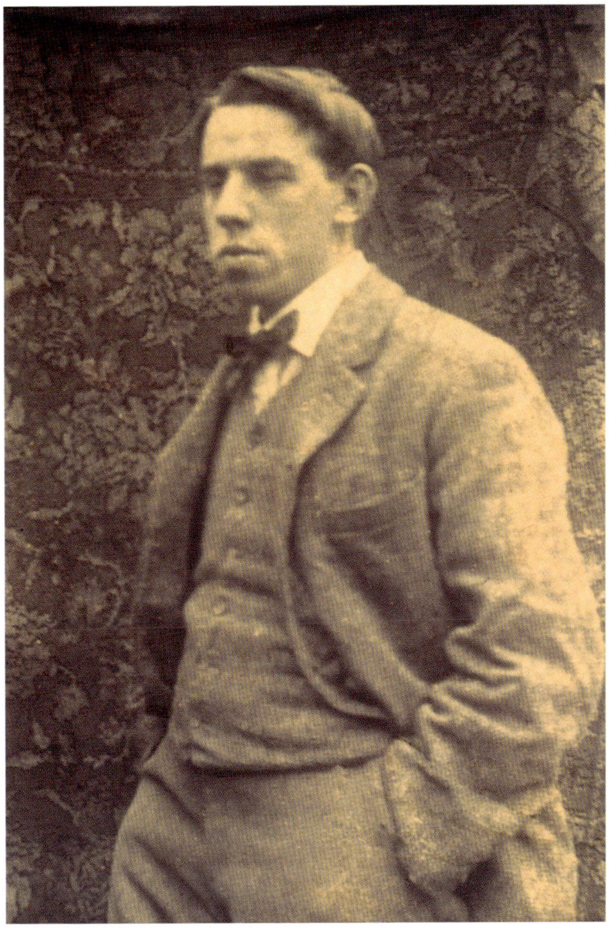

Carey off to Newlyn in 1902

2 DAWN OF GENRE

It was indeed an exciting time, and a very big step for a boy from a small, friendly, Free Church Sabbatarian rural town, where everyone knew everyone else and strangers were viewed with suspicion. But Carey need not have worried because Newlyn was similarly a small, friendly, Free Church Sabbatarian fishing village with a great sense of community which excluded strangers. The main differences were that Newlyn was much warmer than Llandeilo, even in October, and the rich comforting smell of horses and horse manure on the streets on market days in Llandeilo was replaced by the fresh scaly smell of pilchards and mackerel with fish heads and guts littering the beach and cobbled streets of Newlyn when the boats returned from the fishing grounds.

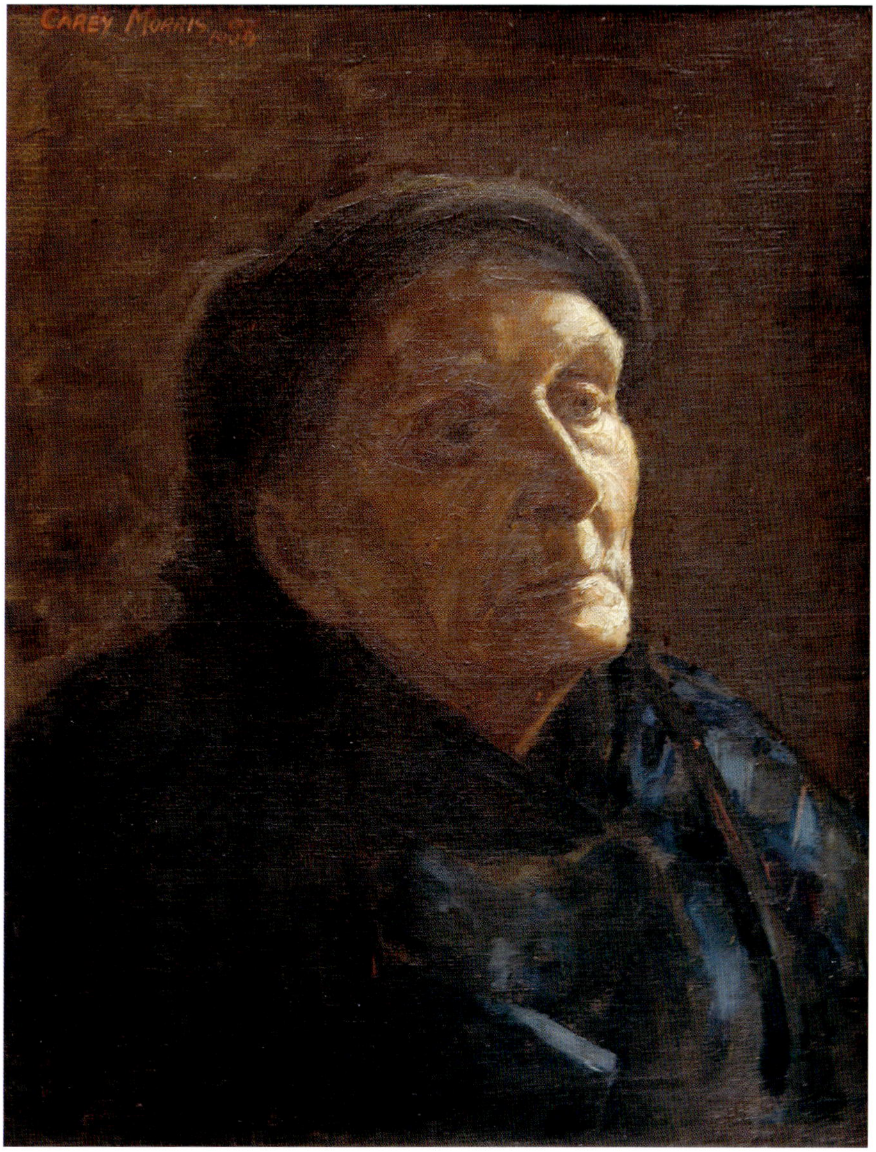

Une Vielle Femme 1909 18½" x 14"

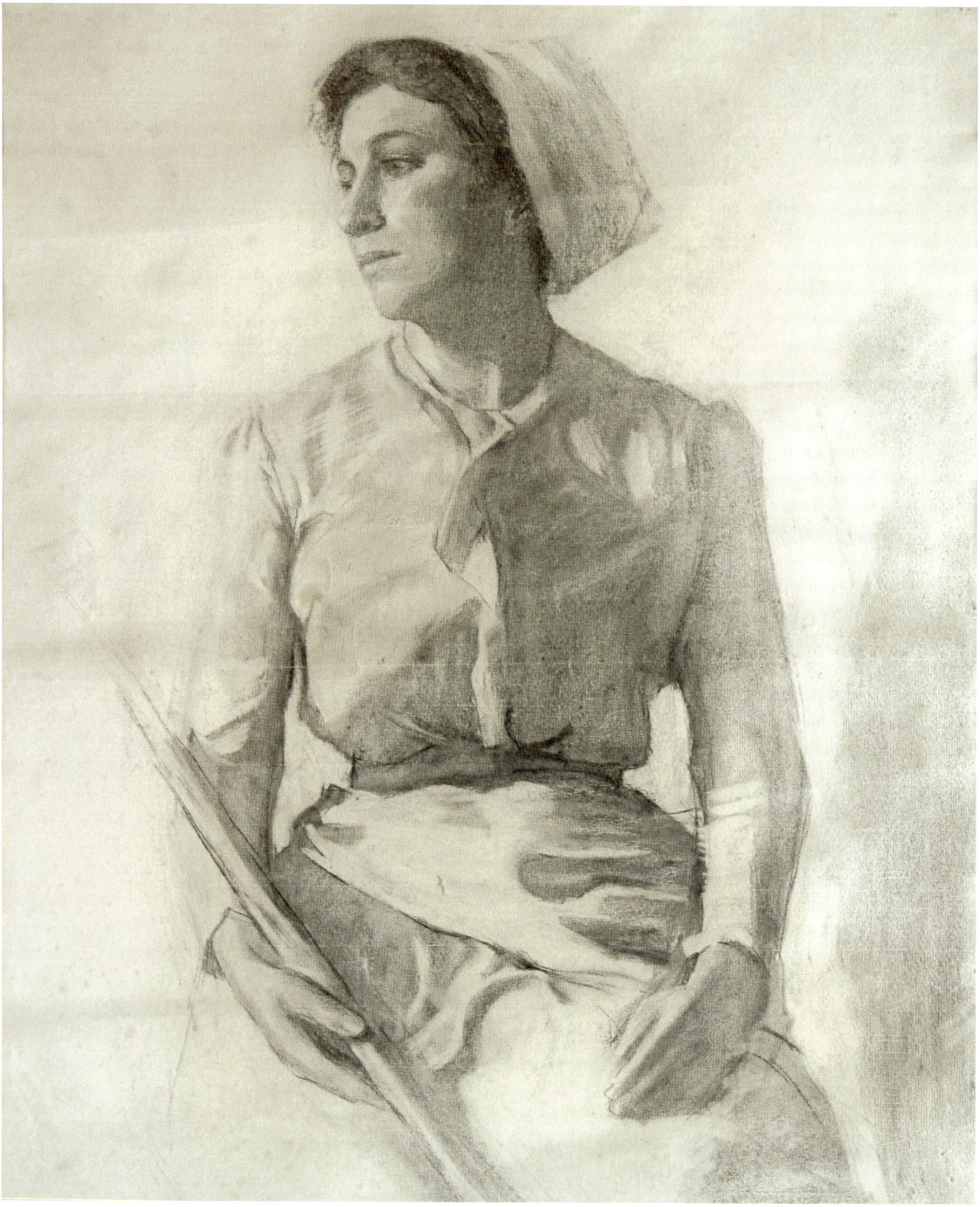

A Housemaid 24" x 18"

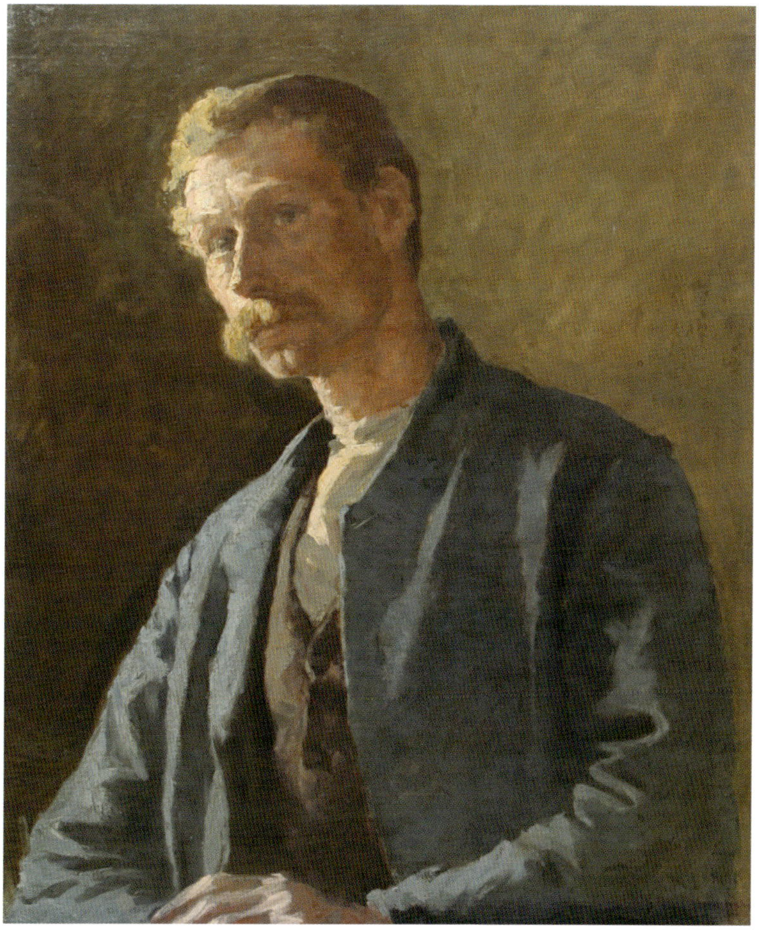

A Farmworker 1902 29½" x 24"

Newlyners were inherently suspicious of strangers who were not fishermen or tin miners, but soon accepted Carey as a fellow Celt, so that, as an artist, he had no difficulty in persuading them to sit for him. However, they were rather surprised at being asked to model in their working or everyday clothes, rather than in their Sunday best, as exemplified by his oil of an old lady (titled *Une Vielle Femme* when exhibited in Paris), his charcoal of *A Housemaid* and two oils – *A Farmworker* and *A Roadmender.*

Newlyn became a second home for Carey, who arrived there with another student, Hereward Tresidder, who was a year younger and hailed from Falmouth. They shared lodgings in Florence Place near Tolcarne Bridge, and became close friends. Most students left Newlyn at Christmas and during the summer many visited the Royal Academy. Carey mentioned in a letter that he spent a most happy Christmas

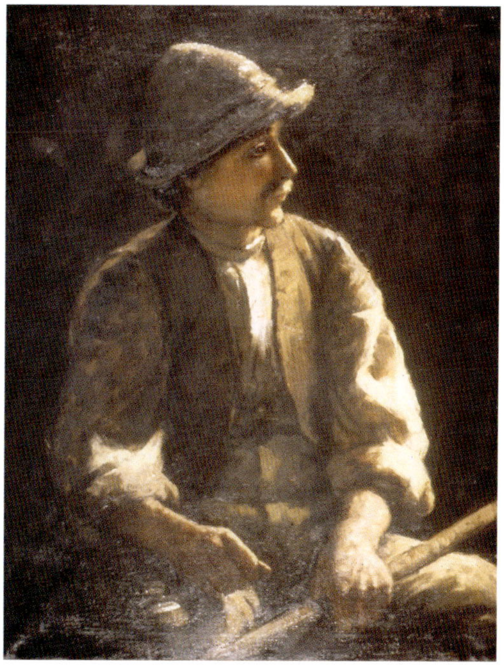

A Roadmender 1903 27½" x 25½"

holiday with the Tresidder family at their home in Park Terrace, Falmouth, and that Hereward produced a small painting of *Carey as a student.*

Carey began his studies with the other students in what he described as the elementary class, which was, in fact, held in a small hut called the 'cast room', where beginners were taught to draw limbs and heads of classical *bronzes cast in plaster.* However, Carey told me that as a result of his study of surface anatomy before going to Newlyn, he was very soon promoted to the next class, which was held in a larger hut where students were taught to draw and paint from living models. It was either here or, more probably, in the third and largest hut, that Carey first met the already accomplished and acclaimed artist, Walter Langley R.I., who

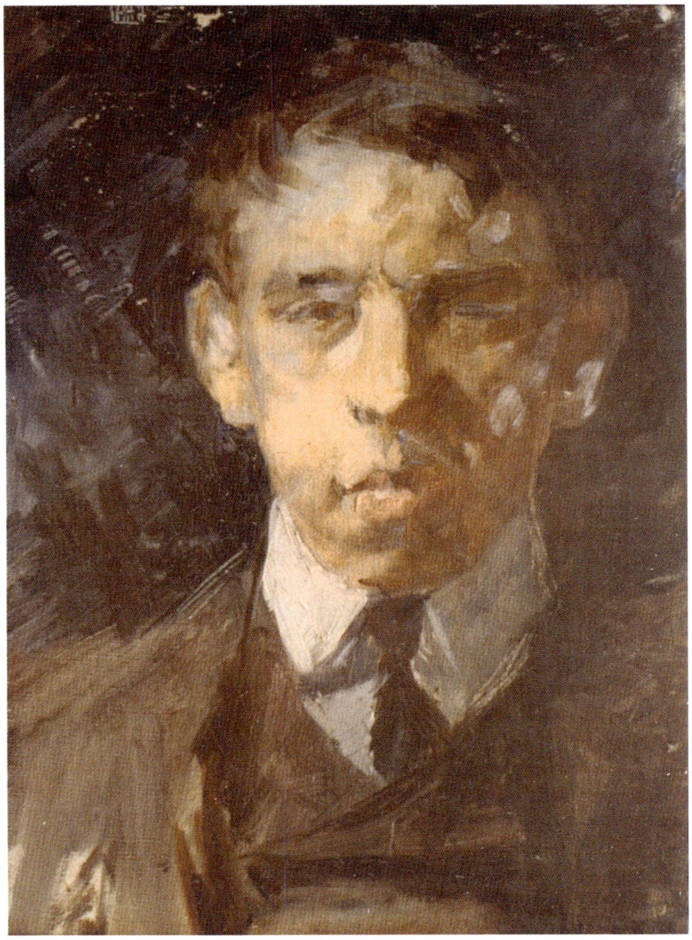

Hereward Tresidder's painting – *Carey Morris* 1907 10" x 8"

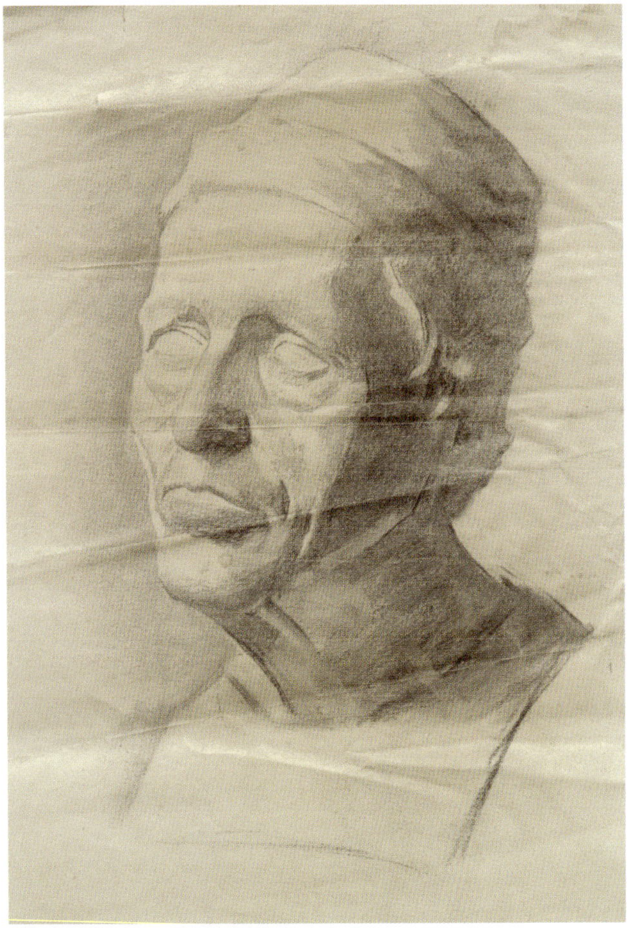

Plaster head from cast room 24" x 18"

was greatly influenced by Bastien-Lepage's *en plein air* work which was a central feature of Impressionism. Carey was later to paint Walter Langley in 1911 and this painting was hung in the Royal Academy but, unfortunately, Walter Langley's painting of Carey is lost.

Langley was 30 years older than Carey and very probably conveyed his great respect for the ordinary hard-working fisher folk of Newlyn to Carey, and this warm feeling for those who toil hard for a living also permeates through much of Carey's work. The students were taught to paint what they saw without any amelioration – the aim being to portray the innate dignity of ordinary working people, thus following the tenets of Courbet's Realist school.

Overseeing the Newlyn School of Painting was

its founder, Stanhope Forbes, who was known as 'The Professor'. It was Forbes who held the whole school together with his personality. The site of this school was originally a five-acre field overlooking Newlyn harbour. It had been donated to the original colony of artists by a Slade graduate, some years before Carey arrived. It became known as 'The Meadow'.

When I last visited Newlyn a few years ago, I found a gate in Trewarveneth Street, marked 'The Meadow, Private', which led up a lane to a cul-de-sac. The Meadow has been largely encroached upon by the gardens of surrounding houses, but it was just possible to see one of Stanhope Forbes' own studios, together with some derelict ramshackle buildings which could have been the remains of the studios where Carey painted, but there was no access to the area.

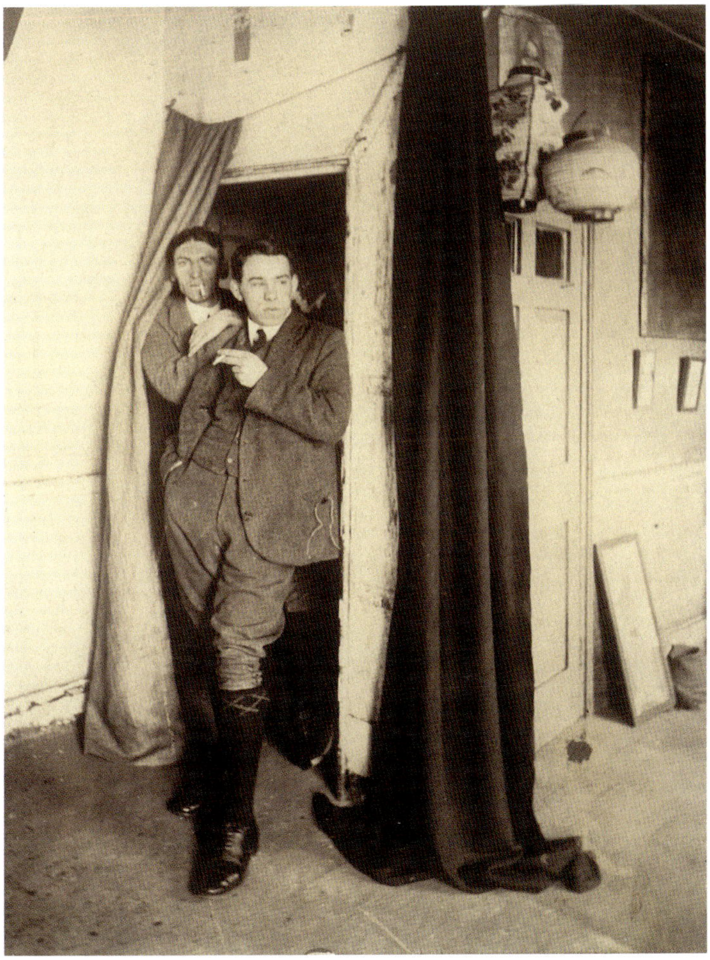

Carey and friend in studio

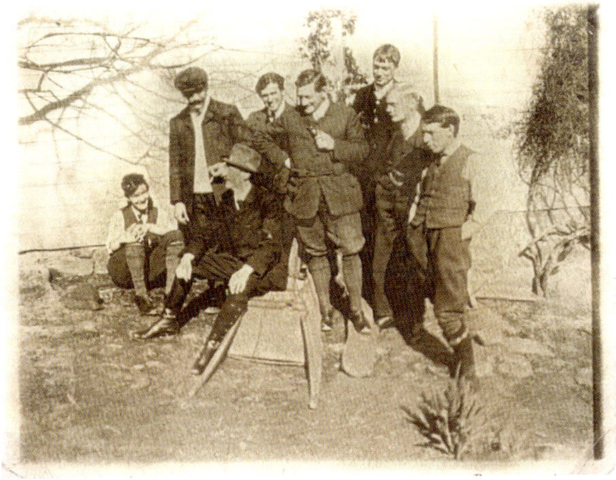

Stanhope Forbes with students

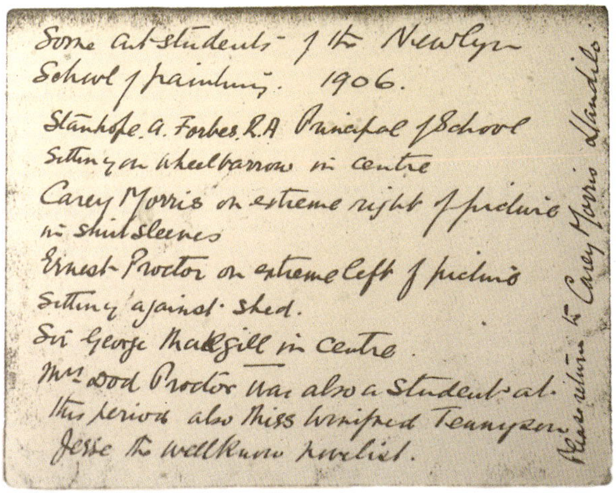

Some art students of the Newlyn
School of painting. 1906.
Stanhope A. Forbes R.A Principal of School
Sitting on wheelbarrow in centre
Carey Morris on extreme right of picture
in shirtsleeves
Ernest Proctor on extreme left of picture
sitting against shed.
Sir George Makgill in centre.
Mrs Dod Proctor was also a student at
this period also Miss Winifred Tennyson
Jesse the wellknown novelist.

Please return to Carey Morris Llandilo

I also took the opportunity to visit Higher Faugan, the house Mr & Mrs Stanhope Forbes built in 1904. It is approached by a half mile long drive and is just outside Newlyn. It is now a country house hotel, but I was shown the large room used as a studio by Forbes and his wife, who was also an artist. Carey and other students were occasionally entertained to tea at Higher Faugan by Mr & Mrs Forbes. In a letter Carey wrote in 1951 to Hereward Tresidder's widow, he says: 'I had intended visiting Cornwall in 1939 but the war put a stop to my plans. I had promised to let Mr Stanhope Forbes know what date I would be going there. I wish I had gone now, just to see

Mr Forbes once again, for he was grand to us all at Newlyn in those days.' Stanhope Forbes was indeed respected and fondly remembered by his students, who numbered at least 200 over the years. He continued painting well into his eighties, as Carey did, and became the *éminence grise* of his school. He died aged 90 in 1947. He had survived his wife by 35 years. Their son had been killed during World War I.

Carey also adds in that 1951 letter to Mrs Tresidder: 'I was very proud of having had dear Hereward as my great friend in those lovely days in Newlyn – times that I can never forget. I so wish that I could live them all over again.'

Incidentally, Stanhope Forbes did not allow his students to sign the paintings they'd made under his or one of his tutors' supervision – this may account for the absence of Carey's signature in some of his Newlyn pictures – though many of his post-Newlyn pictures are also unsigned. In Carey's own hand there is a diagram indicating the colours used on the palette of most of the artists in Newlyn and also the lesser-known St Ives School.

Besides being taught by Stanhope Forbes, Carey was tutored, as already mentioned, by Walter Langley, who had come to Newlyn to paint in 1882, two years prior to Forbes' arrival in Newlyn. Before Carey arrived Langley had already been accorded the supreme honour of being asked, in 1895, to supply a self-portrait to the Uffizi Gallery in Florence, which houses, since the seventeenth century,

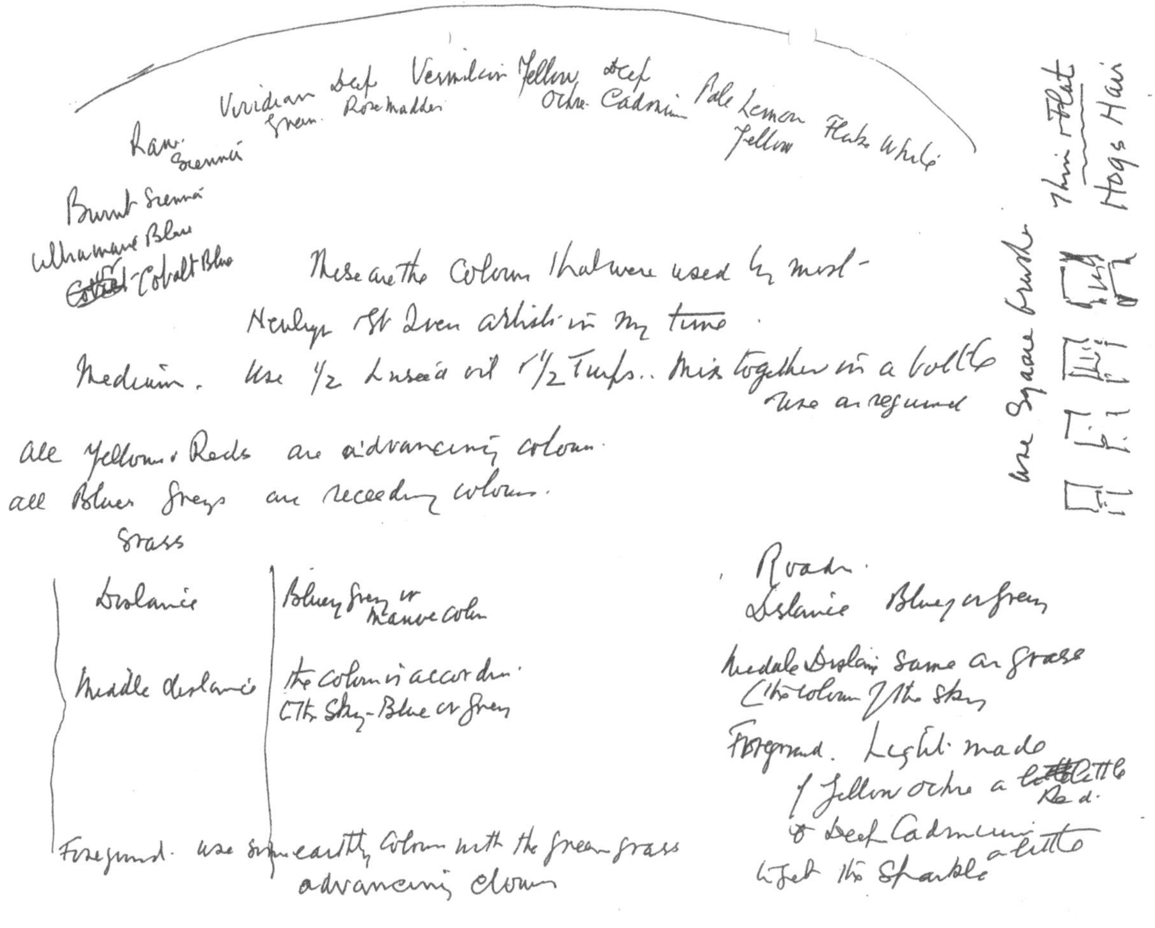

Carey's palette at Newlyn – in his own hand

self-portraits of the greatest internationally renowned artists, including Rembrandt, Raphael and Velázquez; not only that, but Count Leo Tolstoy chose, from paintings by other great artists, a painting by Langley to illustrate the meaning of the term 'true art' in his book *What is Art?*

Other associates of Carey's were Thomas Cooper Gotch, whose art suggests, as well as denotes, and who was known for his allegorical pictures of children, and also his great friend Henry Scott Tuke, the aesthete, whose philosophy, like Carey's, from an artist's point of view, was in accord with that of Rupert Brooke – 'Is there a greater tragedy than the death of a boy, except that he live and grow old?' – for Tuke painted nude figures in seascapes, thereby incurring the wrath of hypocritical prudes of that era. He and Gotch were founder members of the New English Art Club, founded in 1886 as a reaction to the attitude of self-satisfaction at the Royal Academy. The club soon contained the majority of the best painters in the land, including Henry Tonks, who was to teach Carey when he attended the Slade Art School after World War I. Carey also met Sir Alfred Munnings who often visited the Newlyn School and was to become another of Carey's tutors at the Slade in the post-war period.

A new arrival at Newlyn was Ernest Proctor who, as a fellow student, became Carey's close friend, wholeheartedly joining in in the communal social life of the artists of Newlyn. They met at one another's lodgings or in the homes of the married artists to engage in amateur dramatics and to hold musical evenings. Stanhope Forbes was a good pianist; Walter Langley, on his frequent visits, played the banjo; while Carey played the cello. When Alfred Munnings arrived he took charge of the musical evenings and organized a choir, while on other occasions he threw parties and, with his irrepressible vitality, took over the social life of the community, persuading Carey the raconteur and cellist, Ernest Proctor the composer of limericks, and Gotch the talented actor, to whet the palates of the artists of Newlyn.

For Carey, these happy occasions recalled 'nosweithiau llawen' (evenings of informal entertainment) in Llandeilo. It became evident from my conversations with him that, from the very first, he became an active member of the vibrant and varied social life enjoyed by the artists of Newlyn. But, despite all the distractions presenting themselves to a young man who had just left home for the first time, Carey, no doubt aware that he was financially completely dependent on his parents, applied himself diligently to his drawing and painting. In fact, most of his oil paintings which were accepted at the Royal Academy were painted during his pre-war days at Newlyn where he'd remained following the end of his three-year course. Eventually, he took a studio in Cheyne Walk, Chelsea, but the warmth and camaraderie of the Newlyn community drew him back time and again to escape from the cold impersonality and fecklessness of life in the foetid atmosphere of London in those days.

One overcast afternoon in late autumn, whilst wandering around the flat open Cornish countryside near Sennen Cove, some seven miles from Newlyn, Carey found a quiet side road and followed it until he came within sight of the sea, but he branched off into a side lane on the left, which led to a cluster of old buildings seen across some fields. Near this side-turning was a goose pond. Sitting by the side of the pond, tending a flock of geese, was a farm boy. Carey was so enraptured by the peace and tranquillity of the scene, so very close to the ever-threatening Atlantic Ocean, but so quiet and still that day despite its nakedness to the vagaries of the elements, that he was inspired to try to capture its serenity in a painting; this he succeeded in doing. In that beautiful Cornish landscape, Carey must have recognized the same

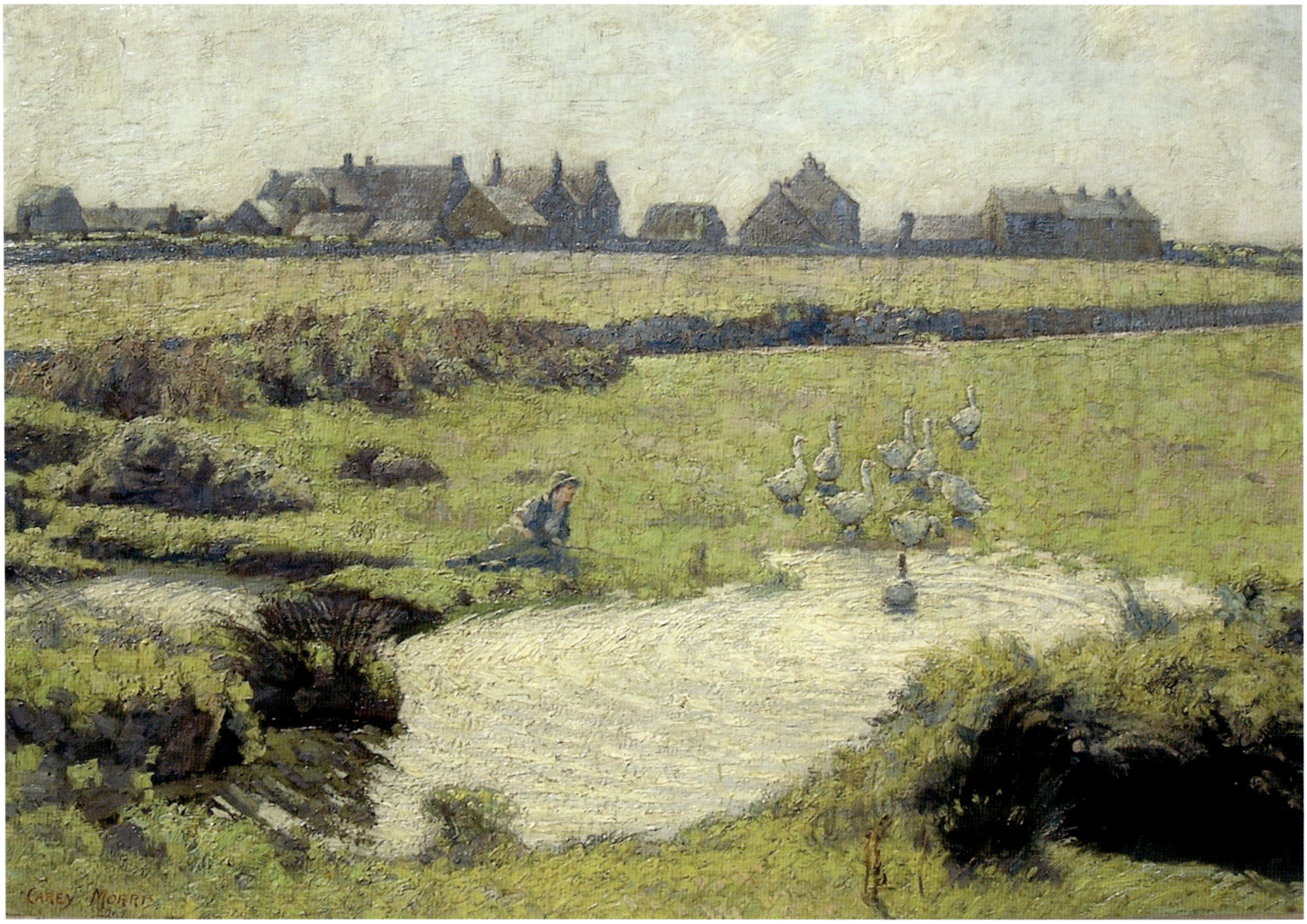

The Goose Pond at Land's End 1905 35½" x 41½"

clarity and intensity of light that illuminates the south-west corner of Wales – that pure light which continues to attract artists to both these ancient Celtic homelands. The result was a memorable painting entitled *The Goose Pond at Land's End* which was later exhibited at the Royal Academy. The largest building seen across the fields in the painting is a farmhouse called Escalls.

In the autumn of 2001 I visited the area and stood at the vantage point where, before World War I, Carey had stood to create his painting . The goose pond had silted up, but the buildings across the fields on the horizon were exactly as they were in the 1900s when Carey had chanced upon the scene. On the extreme left of the painting is the 'Penny-a-Week School' building, next to it Wellfield Farm house, and then comes Escalls Farm house and Manor Farm and on the far right is a group of cottages, all precisely the same as in Carey's painting, thus illustrating his fidelity in depicting the scene, but also much more than that. His artistry enabled him to suggest to the viewer that the year was drawing to a close, the grass had been scorched by the sun and the low hedge and bushes were stunted by salty spindrift. The whole landscape breathed the still serenity of that calm autumn afternoon so long ago.

It is of interest to mention here that soon after Carey painted the goose pond in the early years of the twentieth century, he made one of his frequent visits home to Llandeilo. It was at this time that Edward Thomas, who was to become one of the most influential poets of World War I called upon

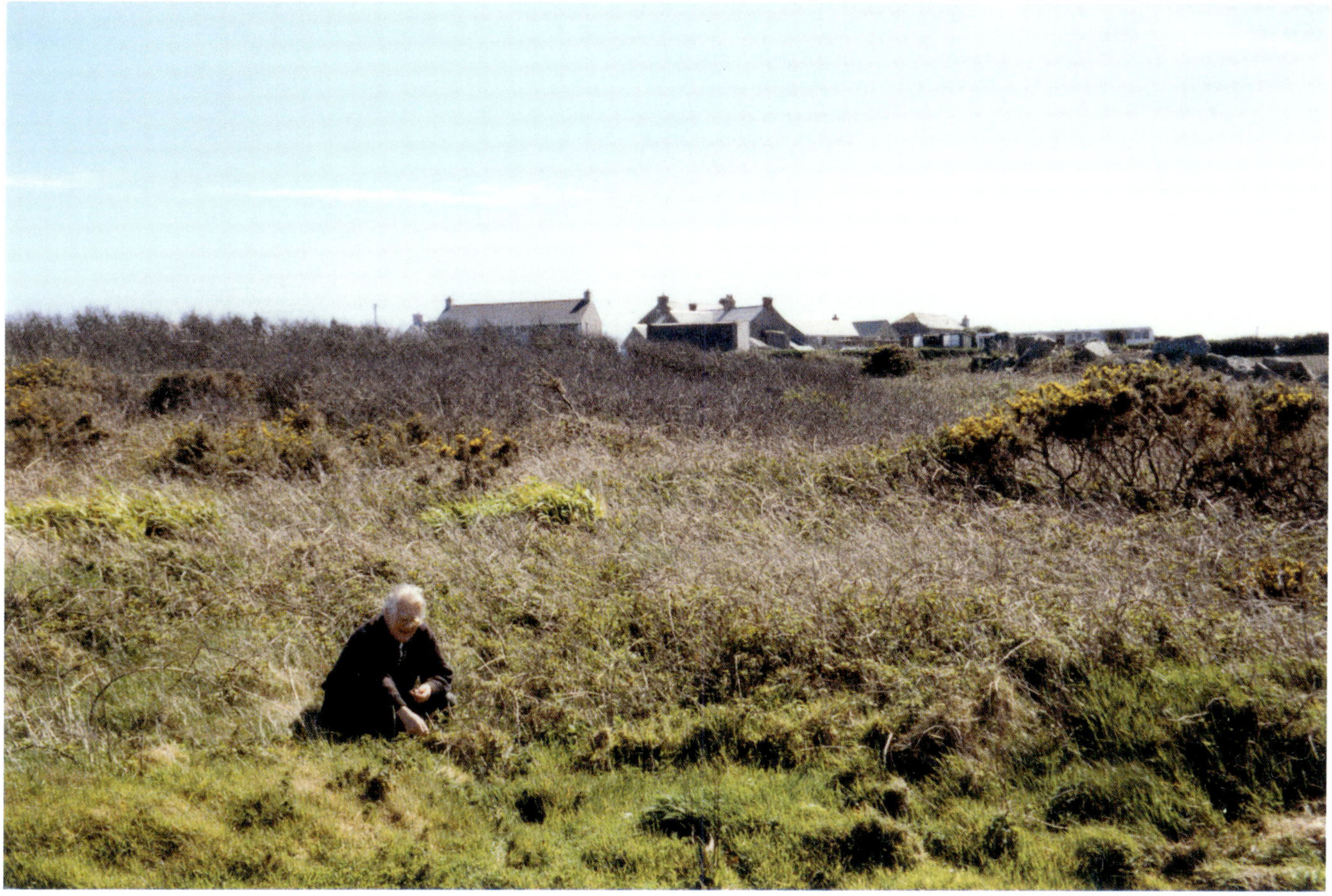

Escalls in 2001

him. Edward Thomas was accompanied by a friend who asked Carey why he preferred to paint geese in Cornwall rather than swans on the River Tywi in Llandeilo. Edward Thomas, who almost always maintained a majestic silence in company, strongly agreed with Carey when he replied that, at that time, 'A real artist had to leave Wales to be trained,' a view Carey reiterated forcibly in the 1920s when he directed the Arts and Crafts section of the Royal National Eisteddfod. (It is also of passing interest to note that it was Edward Thomas who penned the introduction to a volume of poems by John Dyer, whose surname was adopted as a Christian name by Dyer Davies who had taught Carey.)

Carey told me that it was at Escalls farmhouse before World War I that he had painted his oil of an old lady drawing water from a well. It had been accepted for exhibition at the Royal Academy under the title *A Cornish Well* and had attracted such favourable comments that he made at least one half-sized copy and entitled it *A Cornish Peath*. The word 'pŷth' or 'peeth' anglized to 'peath' means an indoor well in Cornish.

I was fortunate to meet the owner of Escalls farmhouse. He knew of the painting because the old lady in the painting was his step-grandmother, but over many years he'd been unable to trace it. He was delighted to learn that it was hanging in my house. He showed me the small lean-to at Escalls farmhouse where Carey had painted *A Cornish Well*.

The lean-to has been considerably altered since Carey was there. His painting shows a small

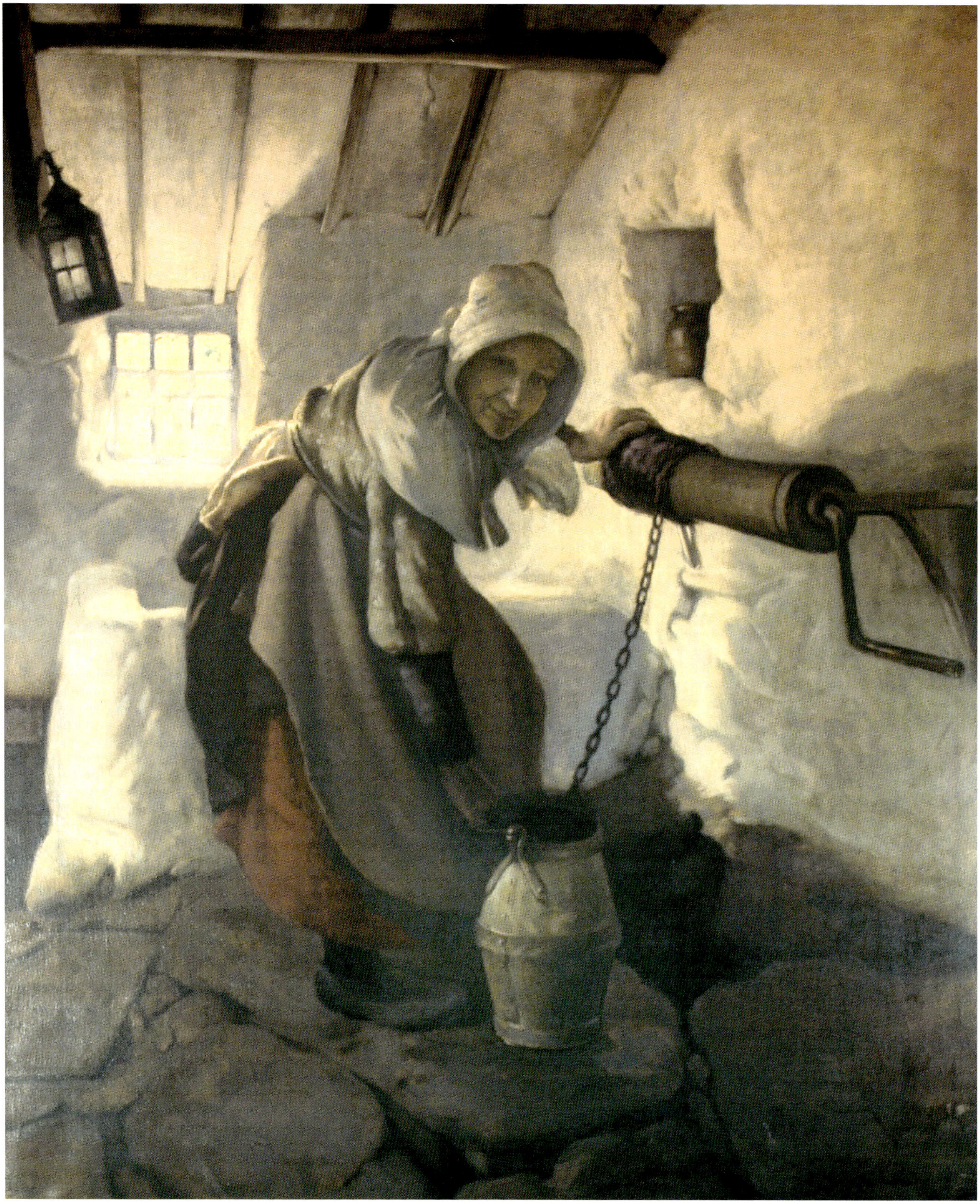

A Cornish Well 1905 57" x 48"

whitewashed lean-to room which has a tiny window with bottle-glazed panes above a heavy trough of Cornish granite. Hanging just above the window is an old lantern and in a deep alcove in the wall is an earthenware jar. The floor is of irregularly-shaped stone slabs and the sloping ceiling is supported by wooden rafters. The well-pitcher or 'stên' is of an unusual shape, and is attached to the hand-operated winch by a chain. The face of the old woman is full of character and she looks straight out of the painting at you. She is wearing a quilted and pleated white bonnet, made by herself, tied under the chin. (Carey so admired her bonnet that she gave him one, which he treasured in his studio for very many years.) She wears a large white shawl-collar over the shoulders and a beige blouse with white spots, the sleeves gathered into close-fitting grey bands from mid-forearm to wrist. Her long woollen skirt is of a deep crimson colour with a black, pleated bustle at the back. Over all this is a thick sackcloth apron and she wears heavy clogs on her feet.

Daylight in the lean-to room comes from three directions – the window seen in the painting and two other sources (not shown in the painting): a very small window in the alcove wall and, to the left of the trough, an outside door, which must have been open to cast the shadow of the winch chain on to the alcove wall. There is another door in the lean-to which leads to the house and it was in this doorway that Carey set up his easel.

When I visited I found that the outside door had been blocked up. With the advent of a mains water supply the well was no longer used. It had been intended to move the trough outside, but it could not be manoeuvred out through the doorway, and so it was tipped end-up down into the well, which was then capped with a concrete slab. The lean-to was reduced in width by demolishing the left-hand wall, as seen from the outside, and building a new wall over part of the concrete cap, so that the well containing the trough is now partly under the new wall and partly outside it. From the outside Carey would have seen the old left-hand wall coterminous with the gable end of the house, as in the 1920s photograph, but the new wall is now further to the right and no longer coterminous with the gable end. Incidentally, the paintings of the Cornish well and of the goose pond go hand-in-hand because the well fed the goose pond which drained into the sea nearby.

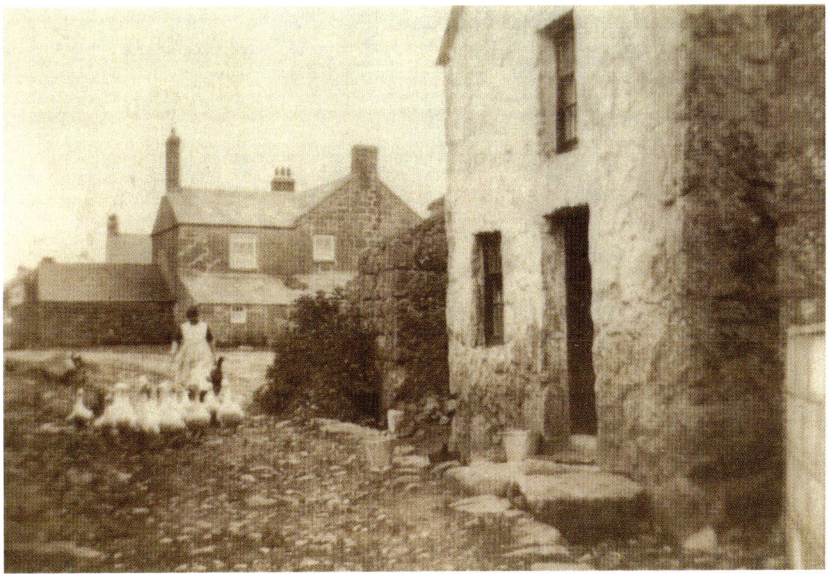

Escalls farmhouse in 1920s

The first of Carey's paintings to be accepted and exhibited at the Royal Academy was the portrait he painted in 1911 of the internationally renowned Walter Langley R.I. – a sensitive man who was a humanitarian. It depressed Langley beyond measure to witness fellow human beings reduced to

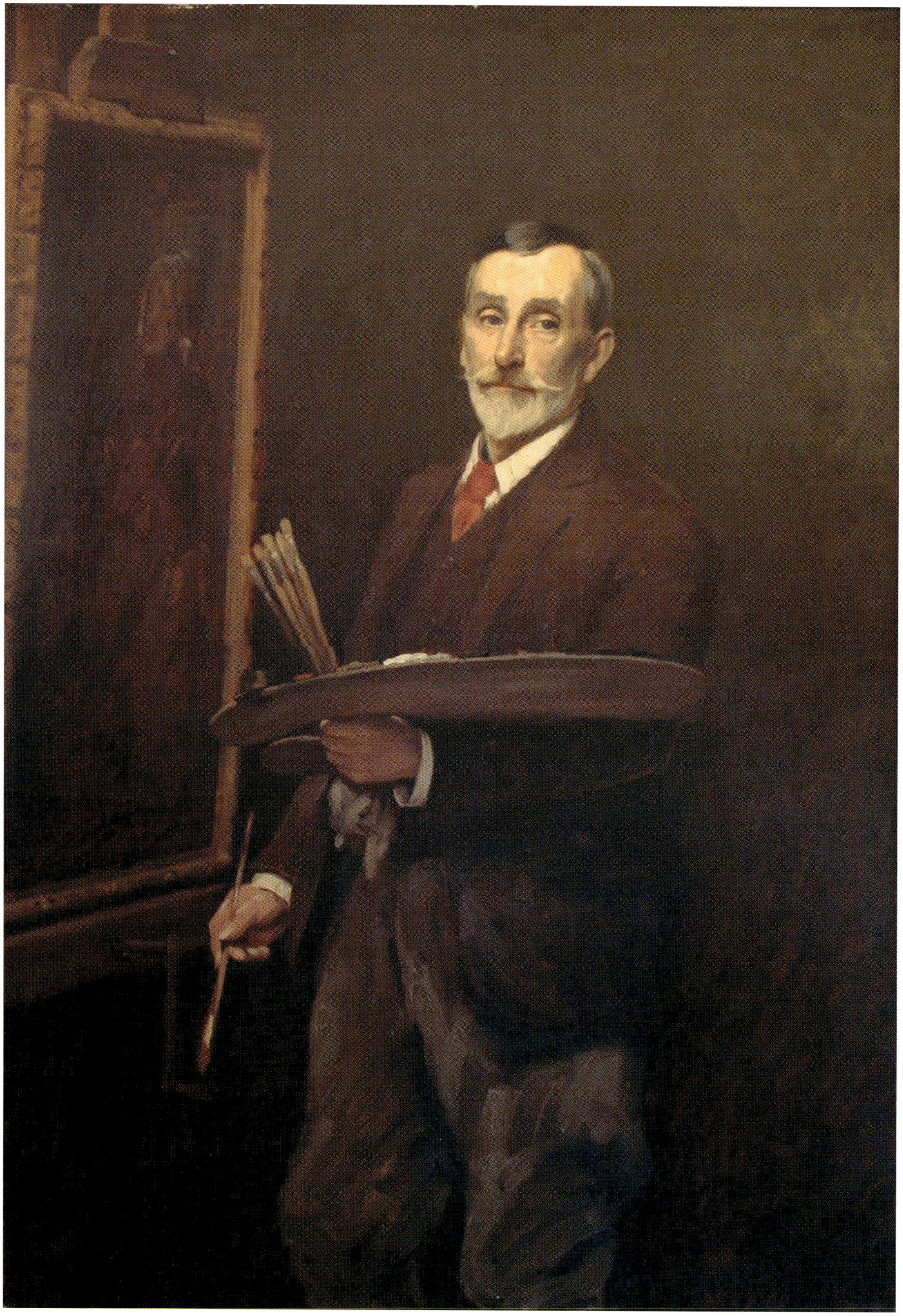

Walter Langley, 1911 59" x 38"

wretchedness by poverty through no fault of their own, for he had seen it all in his home town of Birmingham. He was keenly aware of the underlying gloomy side of his nature, as is evidenced by his 1897 self-portrait for the Uffizi Gallery. The portrait of *Walter Langley* in oils shows a kind face with a sad brooding expression, the eyes looking into the far distance, beyond the observer, though shaded by a wide-brimmed hat. His concern for social reforms did not endear him to the Newlyn artists, any more than his preference for watercolours over oils – though he was a master of both. However, everyone recognized him as a major artist. Langley was small, trim and nimble and, as Carey depicted him, he sported a white, neatly-trimmed van Dyke beard, in contrast to his full jet-black beard in the *Uffizi portrait* painted 14 years previously. But, in addition to portraying Langley's physical characteristics meticulously, Carey also succeeded in conveying in the facial expression Langley's sensitive and compassionate nature. He painted him at his easel wearing a red tie and whilst putting the finishing touches to an already framed painting.

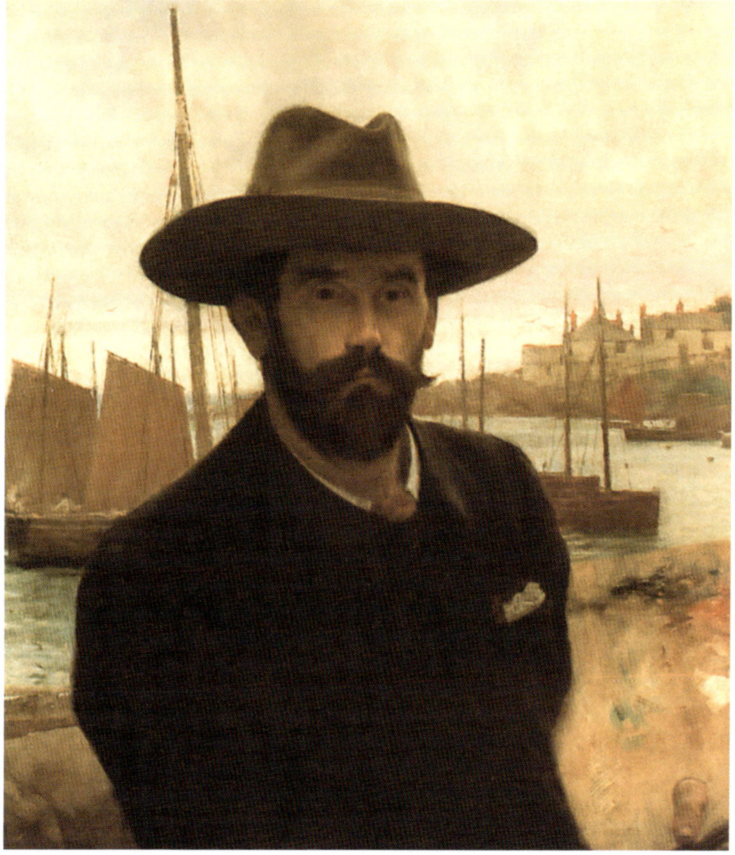

Walter Langley – Uffizi portrait 1897 30½" x 25"

In Newlyn Carey had only to step outside his lodging in Florence Place and, in a few yards at Tolcarne Bridge, he would be at the sea wall where on a stormy day a few dozen people would gather to watch and dodge the angry waves

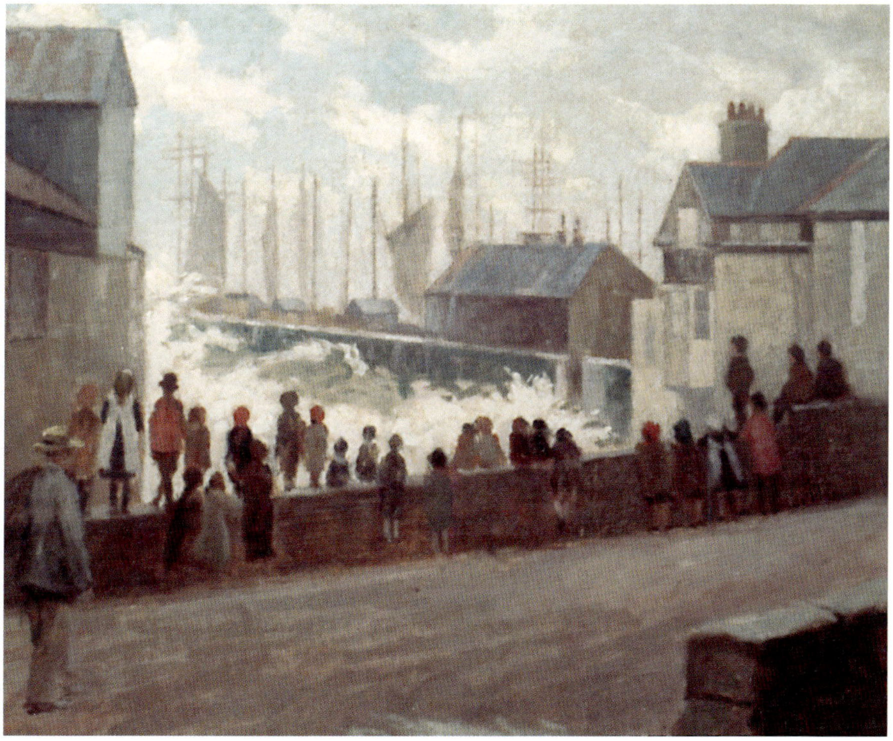

Storm at Tolcarne Bridge 1904 34" x 39½"

frothing as they crashed with a booming roar against the wall. Not surprisingly, Carey captured this dramatic scene on canvas, just as the waves were about to vent their fury, and he called the oil painting *Storm at Tolcarne Bridge*. Sadly, the thrill of dodging waves as they crash over the wall is now denied to young Newlyners, since large boulders have been strategically placed in the estuary to serve as breakwaters. Also, within easy walking distance of Carey's lodgings at Florence Place was *The Slipway* or 'Slip', which could be reached by skirting the harbour past the fish market on the Fradgan, and thence up the Strand. In Carey's time the Slipway was the boundary between that part of Newlyn surrounding the estuary of the River Coombe at Tolcarne, and the upper or cliff part overlooking the harbour. After the construction of a new road in the 1900s, the two parts of Newlyn became one. In his wanderings Carey came across two local scenes that appealed to him and he portrayed them in two charming paintings which evoke the peaceful unhurried pace of rural life – *Washing Day* and *Pastoral Scene*.

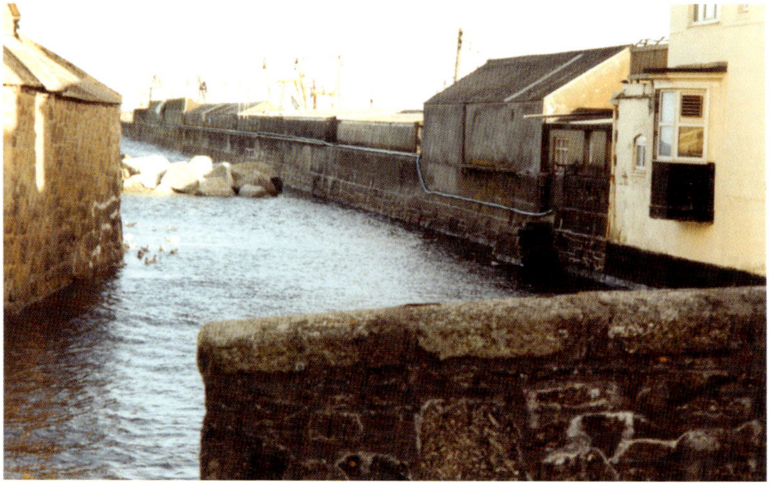

Tolcarne Bridge today

At this time he was also aware of the demanding, life-threatening and harsh existence of the men whose livelihood depended on the sea, and he succeeded in conveying these sober realities in sensitive charcoal and oil studies of the *Newlyn Fishermen*. In complete contrast he painted a striking pensive head and shoulders studio portrait of a *Newlyn model*.

The mutual friendship and respect between Carey and the Newlyners extended well beyond his student days and the first decade of the twentieth century. Carey's power of revealing several moods – both of sitter and artist within one picture – became apparent, though Sir Kyffin Williams always maintained that a portrait often revealed the mood of the *artist* rather

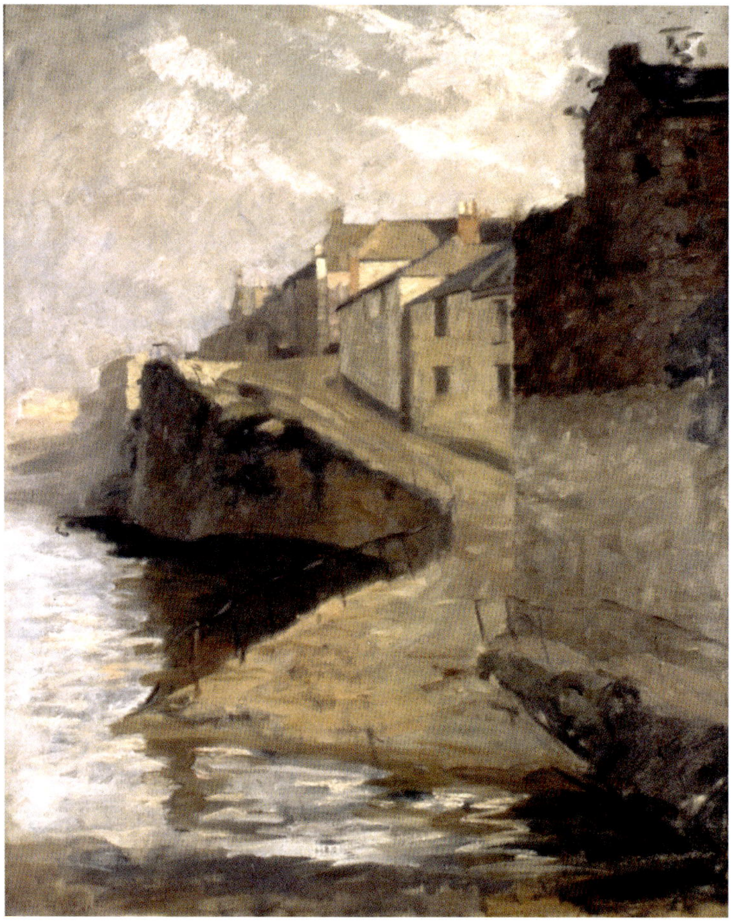

The Slipway 1905 24" x 20"

than the sitter. Carey still retained access to studios in Newlyn, though he also maintained studios in London and his beloved Llandeilo.

He was commissioned to paint a portrait of the poet and writer *Sir Lewis Morris* in 1906. Carey and Sir Lewis were good friends and claimed kinship. Carey often visited Sir Lewis at his Georgian mansion in Llangunnor, near Carmarthen and they frequently met in London as well. Sir Lewis Morris was to the fore in founding and funding the University College of Wales at Aberystwyth. His poetry, which distils in words the mysterious and magical essence of a place, the *genius loci*, was extremely popular. He was a friend of Lord Tennyson and would have succeeded him as Poet Laureate had not Queen Victoria vetoed the offer of appointment because he had a common-law wife! Carey's portrait seems to evince a certain sadness of the eyes in a dignified and somewhat aloof countenance.

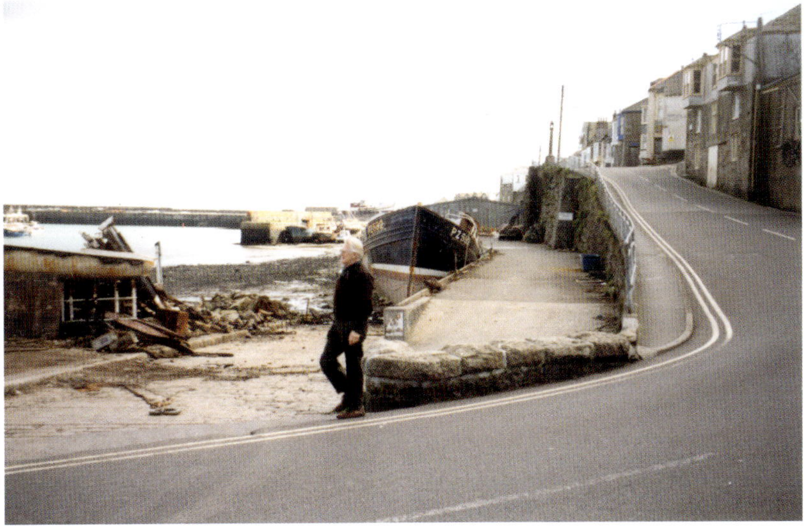
The Slipway today

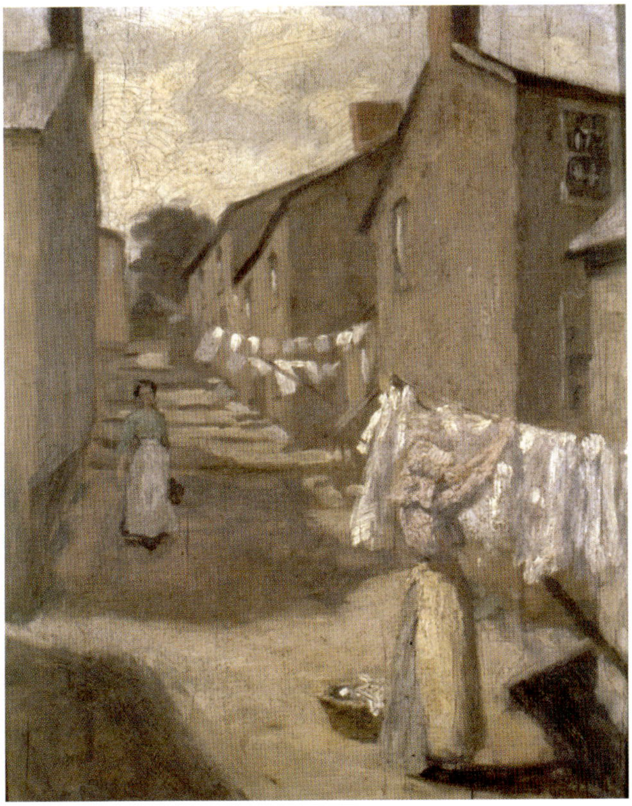
Washing Day 1905

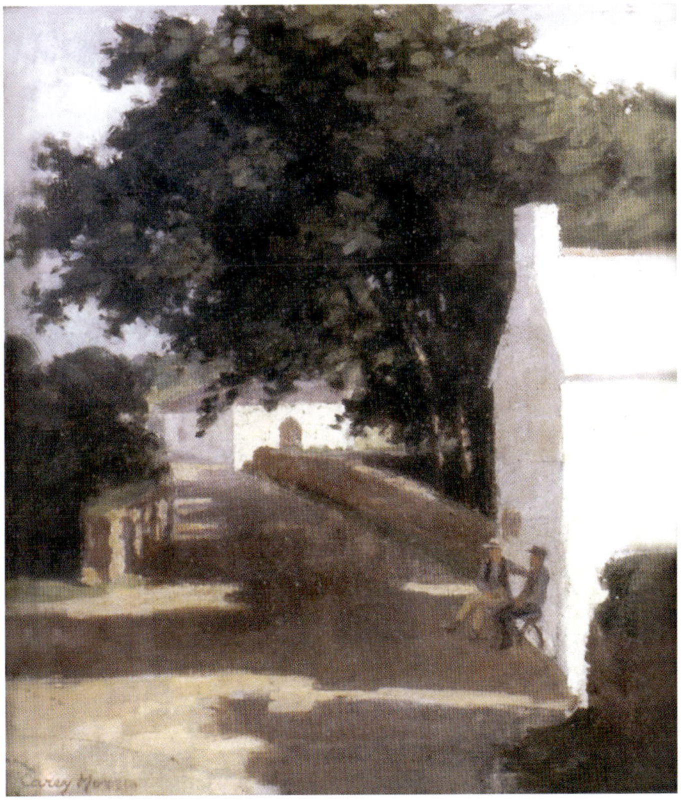
Pastoral Scene 1905

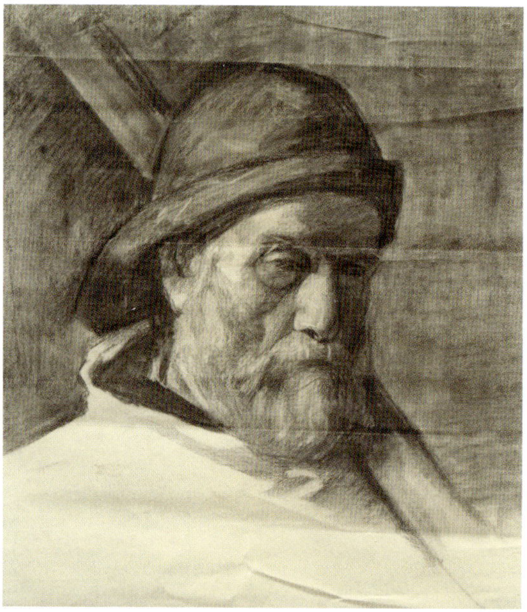

Newlyn Fisherman, charcoal 24" x 18"

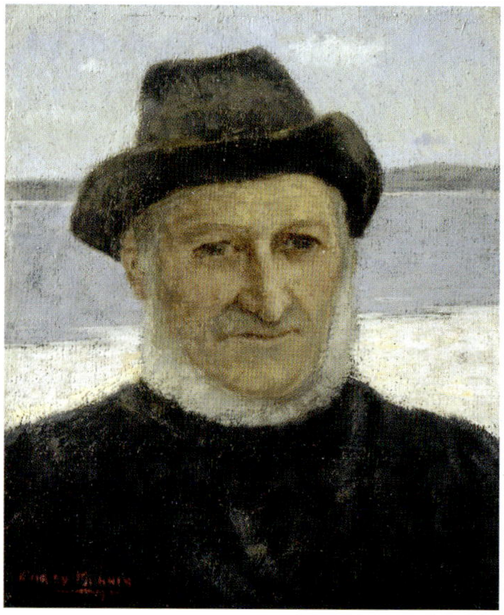

Newlyn Fisherman, oil 12½" x 10½"

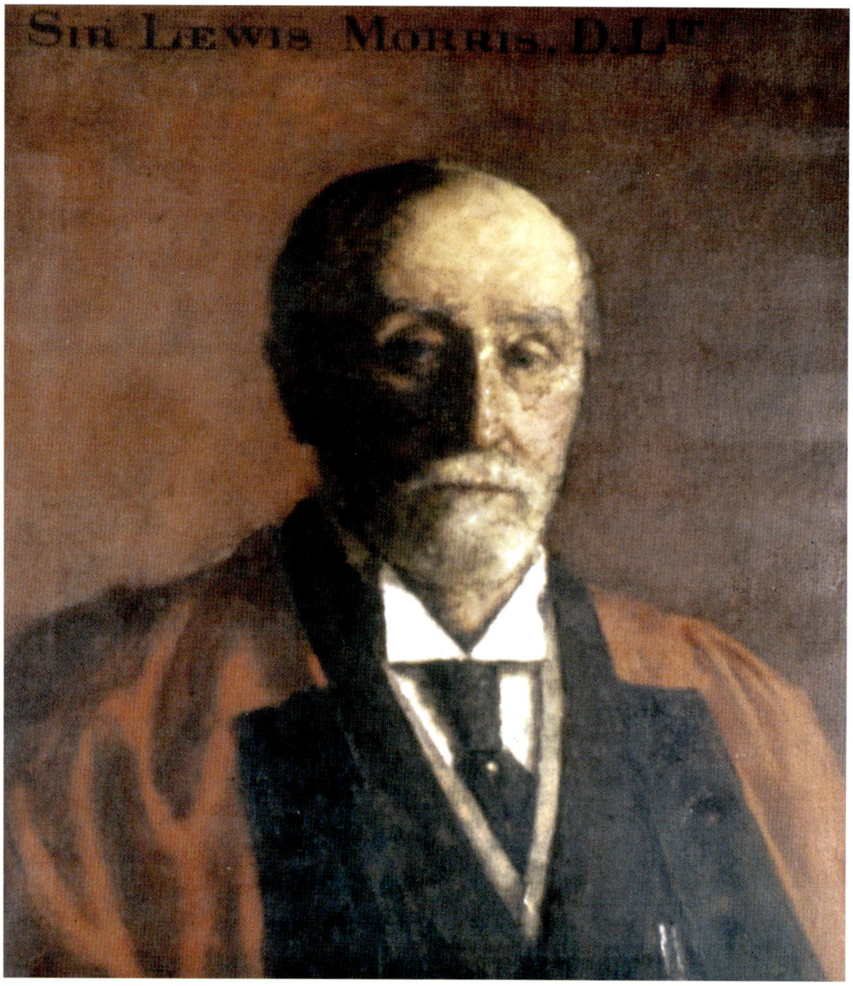

Sir Lewis Morris 24" x 20½"

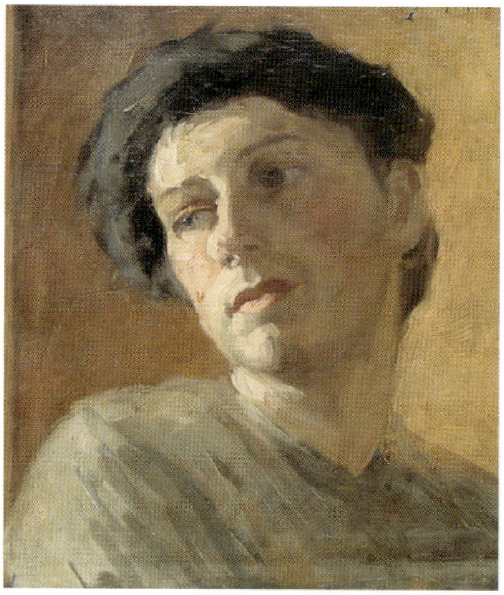

Newlyn model 14½" x 12"

Another important commission at this time was for a portrait of Brigade-Surgeon Lieutenant-Colonel Edward Hopkins who'd had a distinguished army career. In the second Anglo-Afghan War (1878–80) he accompanied General Roberts (later Field Marshal Lord Roberts) on the memorable 320-mile march from Kabul to Khandahar. As reported in *The Welsh Medical Gazette* (winter 1971), Brigade-Surgeon Hopkins was a descendant of John Jones of Myddfai, who was reputed to be a descendant of the Physicians of Myddfai. The description beneath Carey's portrait of the Brigade-Surgeon states: 'Presented to Brigade-Surgeon Lt Col. Edward Hopkins, Carreg Cennen, Llandeilo in recognition of valuable medical services readily and gratuitously rendered for a great many years. June 13, 1908.'

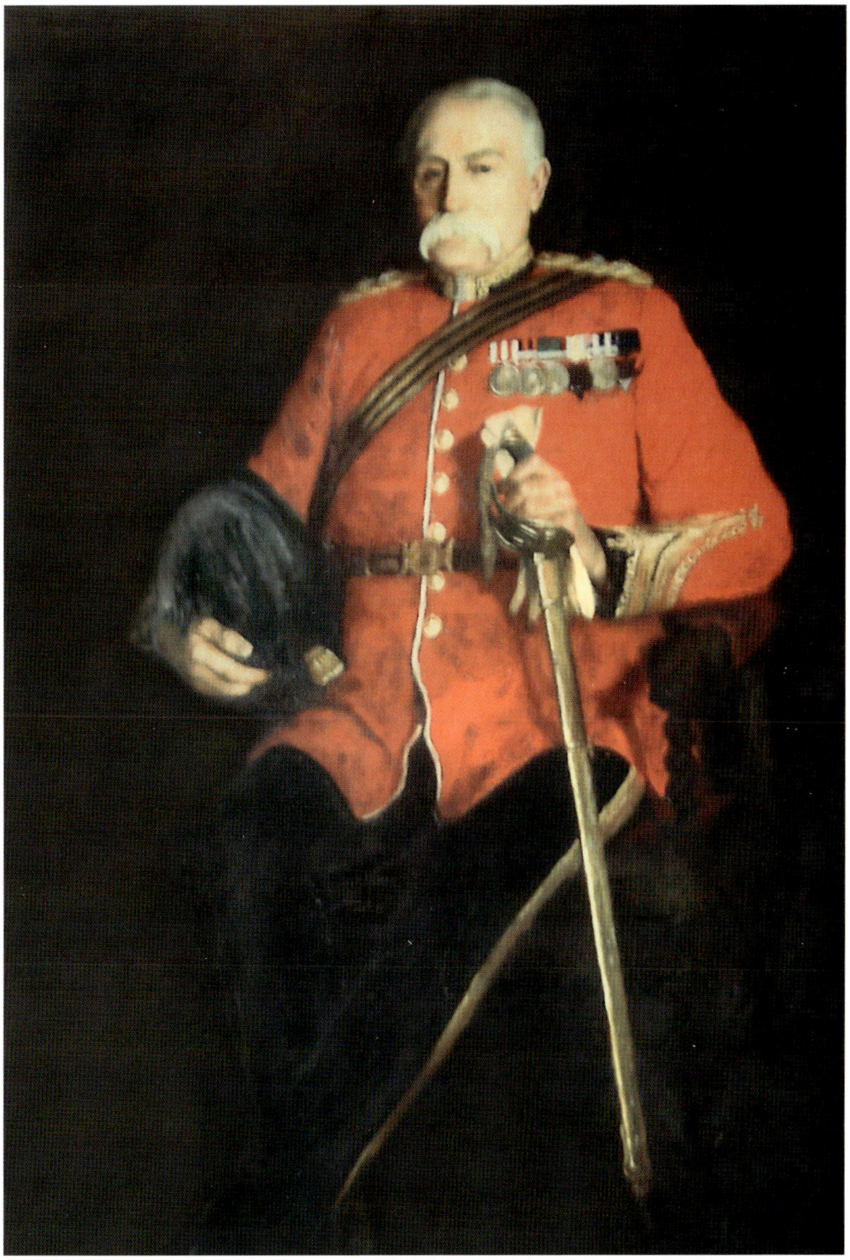

Brigade-Surgeon Lieutenant-Colonel Edward Hopkins 1908 80" x 57"

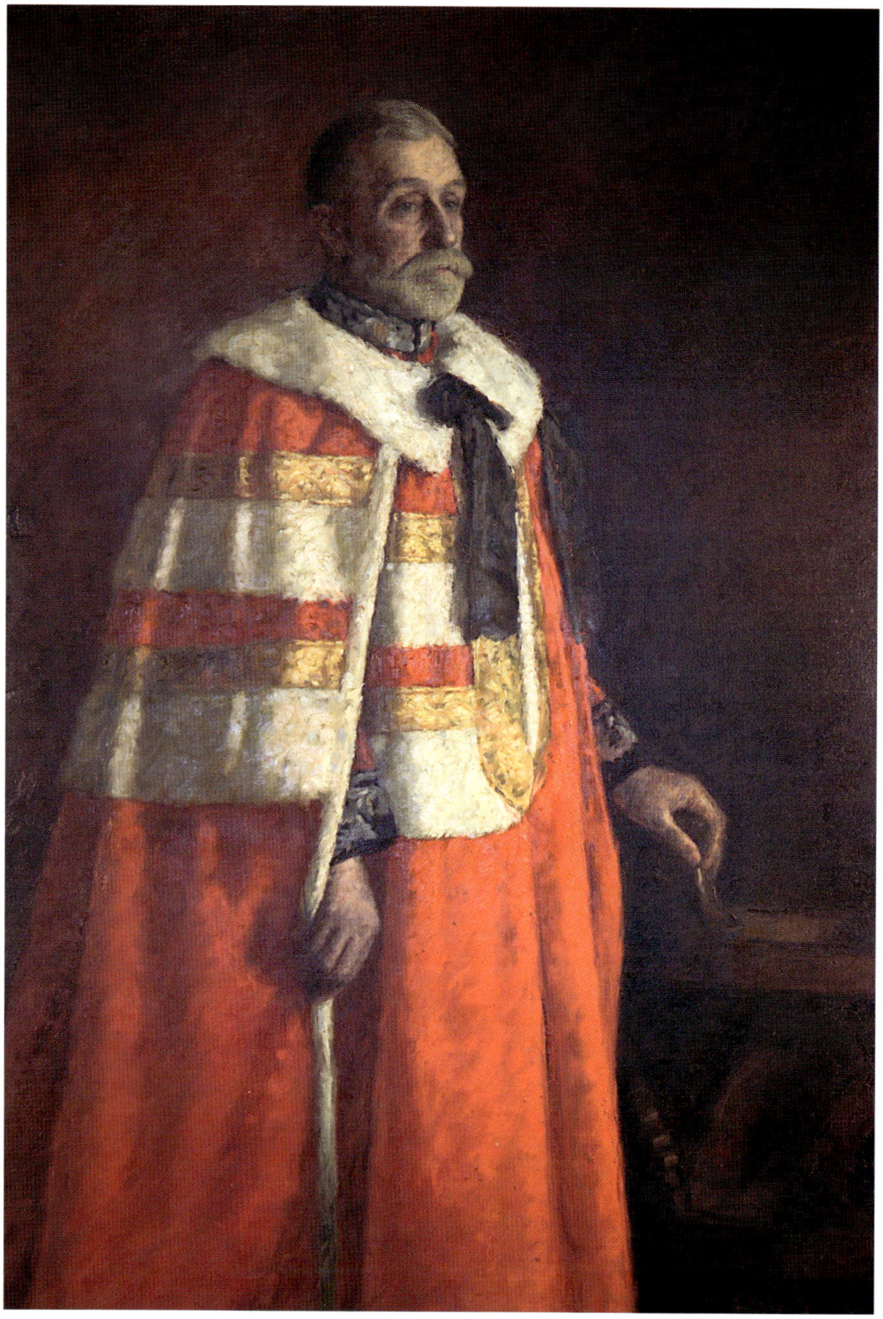

Lord Glantawe 60" x 48"

Carey was also commissioned in the 1900s to paint a portrait of the first *Lord Glantawe*. He'd been knighted in 1881 and created a peer in 1906 in recognition of his 30 years of public service. He was MP for Carmarthen Boroughs on two occasions, 1882–6 and 1895–1900, President of the Royal Institution of South Wales and an honorary Freeman of Swansea, and became the High Sheriff of Glamorgan. Carey portrayed him wearing the robes of a baron, consisting of a mantle of fine scarlet cloth with two bands of white ermine; the cape is furred with 'miniver pure', and two strips of black fur. Carey portrays him as a serious, but kindly-looking, white-bearded man. The portrait can be seen

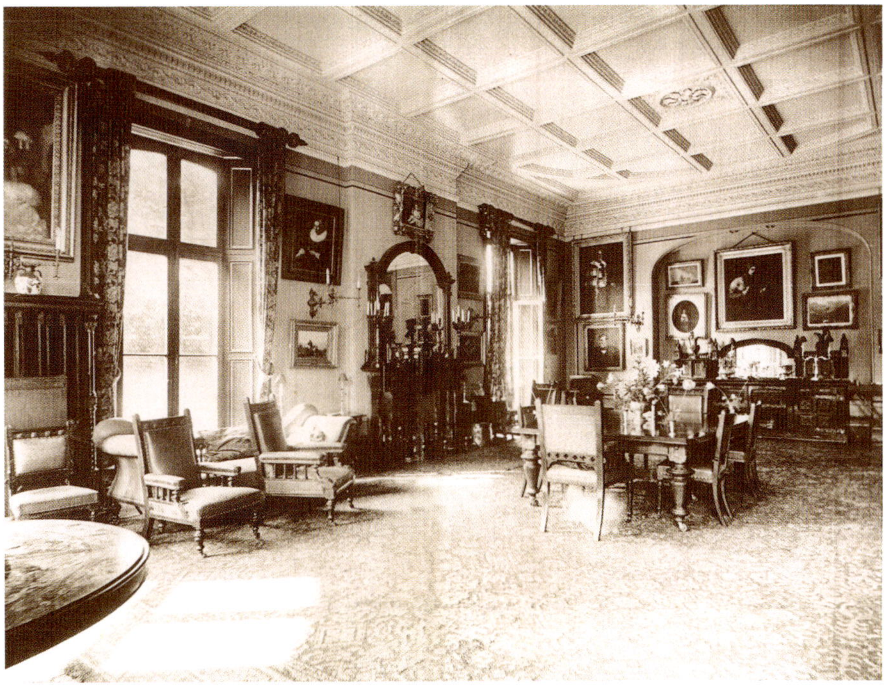

The Grange, West Cross, Swansea

in the photograph to the right of the French window in the spacious dining room, which boasted five similar French windows at his home at The Grange, West Cross, Swansea. Unfortunately, the house was demolished in 1947. I have traced this oil painting to Canada where its proud owner is Lord Glantawe's great-granddaughter.

In 1906, at Llangwm, south Pembrokeshire Carey painted *A Welsh Fisherwoman*, sometimes known as 'The Llangwm Lady'. In those days Llangwm was a small village in a sequestered narrow inlet near the smugglers' house at Black Tar on the western bank of the Western Cleddau, just above Beggar's Reach. Villagers, thought to be descendants of the raiding Vikings, later found themselves in the midst of the multitudes of Flemings imported by Henry I and planted in south Pembrokeshire to displace the native Welsh. As a result, the people of Llangwm kept to themselves and did not welcome outsiders – in fact, young boys were encouraged to throw stones at strangers. Carey must have created a favourable impression in that insular environment, since this was the first time that any Llangwm woman had consented to sit for an artist. Women went out to fish while the men did the housework and often took the name of their wives. The last surviving member of the remarkable Llangwm fisherwomen died in 1946.

Carey told me that the subject of his painting was a Mrs Evans and that she would get up at four in the morning to walk the 35 miles each way, if necessary, to Carmarthen, to sell the fish she had caught the day before. He had also heard that one of these fisherwomen was a friend of the royal family and when the royal yacht visited Milford Haven, she would be entertained on board.

A Welsh Fisherwoman was exhibited at the Royal Academy and portrays a woman with a direct, steady gaze, which hints at knowledge she knows the observer lacks. The arched eyebrows in her long face seem to emphasize her quizzical, serene expression, while her neck betrays her age. Her hands are strong and veined and there is a wedding ring on her left ring finger. The left hand, clasped over the right hand, shows divergence of the little finger from the other fingers which some might interpret as a sign of her strong individuality.

Her black wide-brimmed hat, resembling a somewhat flattened bowler hat, is perched squarely on top of her head. Her delicate loose-fitting, spotted mauve, muslin shawl is worn over her shoulders and draped over the back, and is tucked into the light bodice of her coarse, striped flannel, black dress

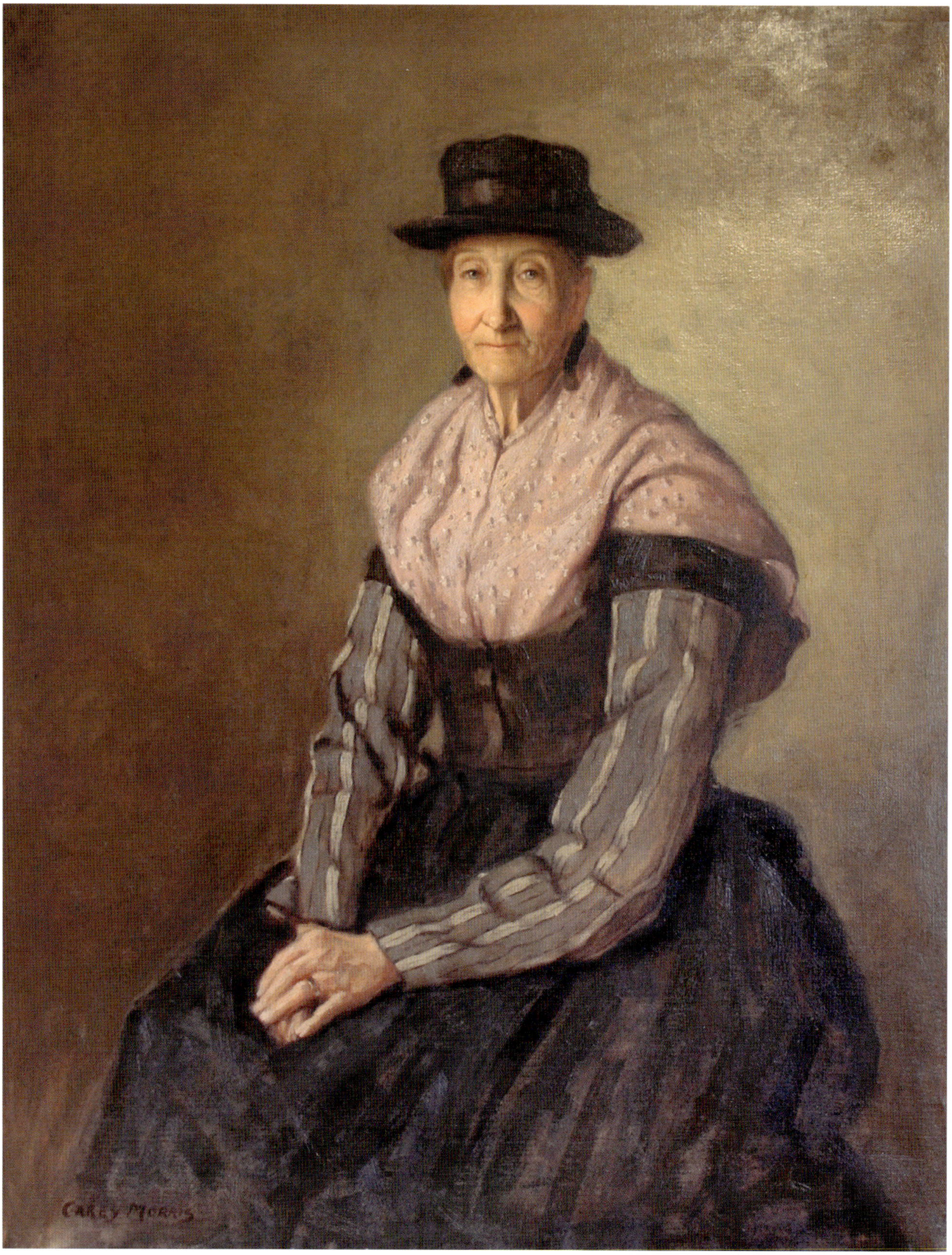

A Welsh Fisherwoman 50" x 40"

which has long tapered grey and white striped sleeves. A black woollen apron is worn over the skirt of the dress, and is tied around her waist and secured by a knotted bow in front.

It was during one of his frequent visits to Llandeilo, accompanied by his fiancée, Miss Jessie Phillips, that Carey was inspired in 1910 to make a preliminary sketch of *Welsh Weavers* before embarking on the creation of his most famous painting, which became known on both sides of the Atlantic. The painting was adopted as a calendar by the Anglo-American publishing company and was seen by millions. *Welsh Weavers* merits detailed description. It shows two members of the Edwards family working at a spinning wheel and loom. Carey was the only Welsh artist to create large-scale paintings depicting folk-life in Wales at this time, and this oil painting is large by any standards (56" x 44"). Carey's commitment to 'Y Werin' (honest, skilled Welsh craftspeople) is evident in his loving, yet unsentimental, presentation of his subjects, as in *Welsh Weavers*, he reflects the commitment of his Newlyn friends to the Cornish fisherfolk. This painting is considered to be *the* definitive large-scale oil painting which seeks to bestow a worthy crown of recognition on an aspect of Welsh rural life from a past era. His Newlyn training had led him to paint such unidealized and contemporary scenes, much like Courbet.

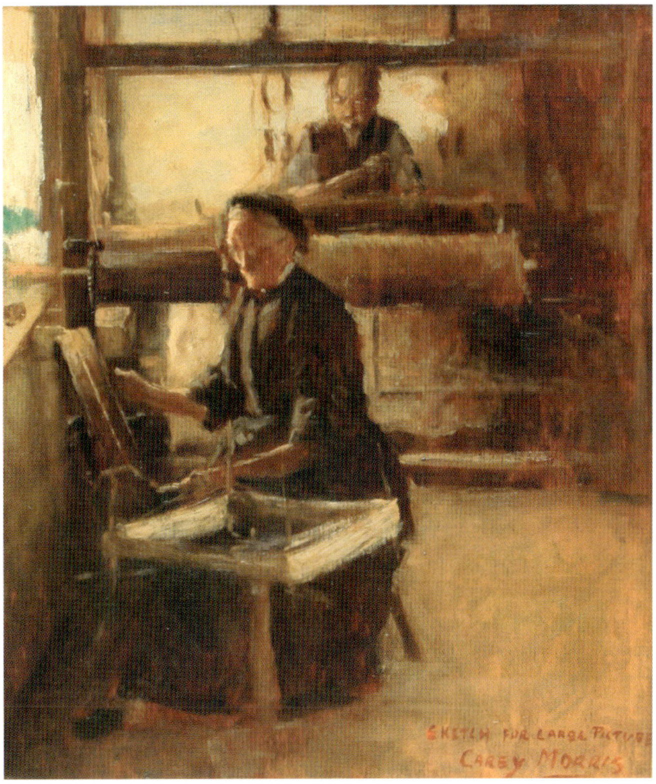

Welsh Weavers, sketch 13" x 11½"

About a mile from Carey's Llandeilo studio, the Edwards family had their workroom at 3, Factory Row, Rhosmaen, Llandeilo, and it was there that Carey painted *Welsh Weavers*. The concentration of the spinner and the weaver is evident in their faces, each completely engrossed in the different rhythms of their patterns of work. The sunlight shining through the window is reflected on their foreheads and glints on their metal spectacle frames. It reveals the lines on the old lady's face which, together with the wrinkled skin, especially on her left forearm, gives an impression of her age (she was over 80) while, at the same time, highlights the rich crimson colour and texture of the front edges of her shawl. Carey was a superb draughtsman as well as a realist. For a detailed description of *Welsh Weavers* see Appendix I.

The Edwards family made beautiful woollen 'carthenni' (bedspreads), shawls and flannels to sell in Llandeilo and other local markets. The family had been weavers since about 1750 and, although power looms arrived in Wales in the 1830s, the Edwards family continued with their handlooms. (Interestingly, a man usually did the weaving and a woman the spinning – hence the term spinster in use since the fourteenth century; the word did not come to mean an unmarried woman until the seventeenth century.)

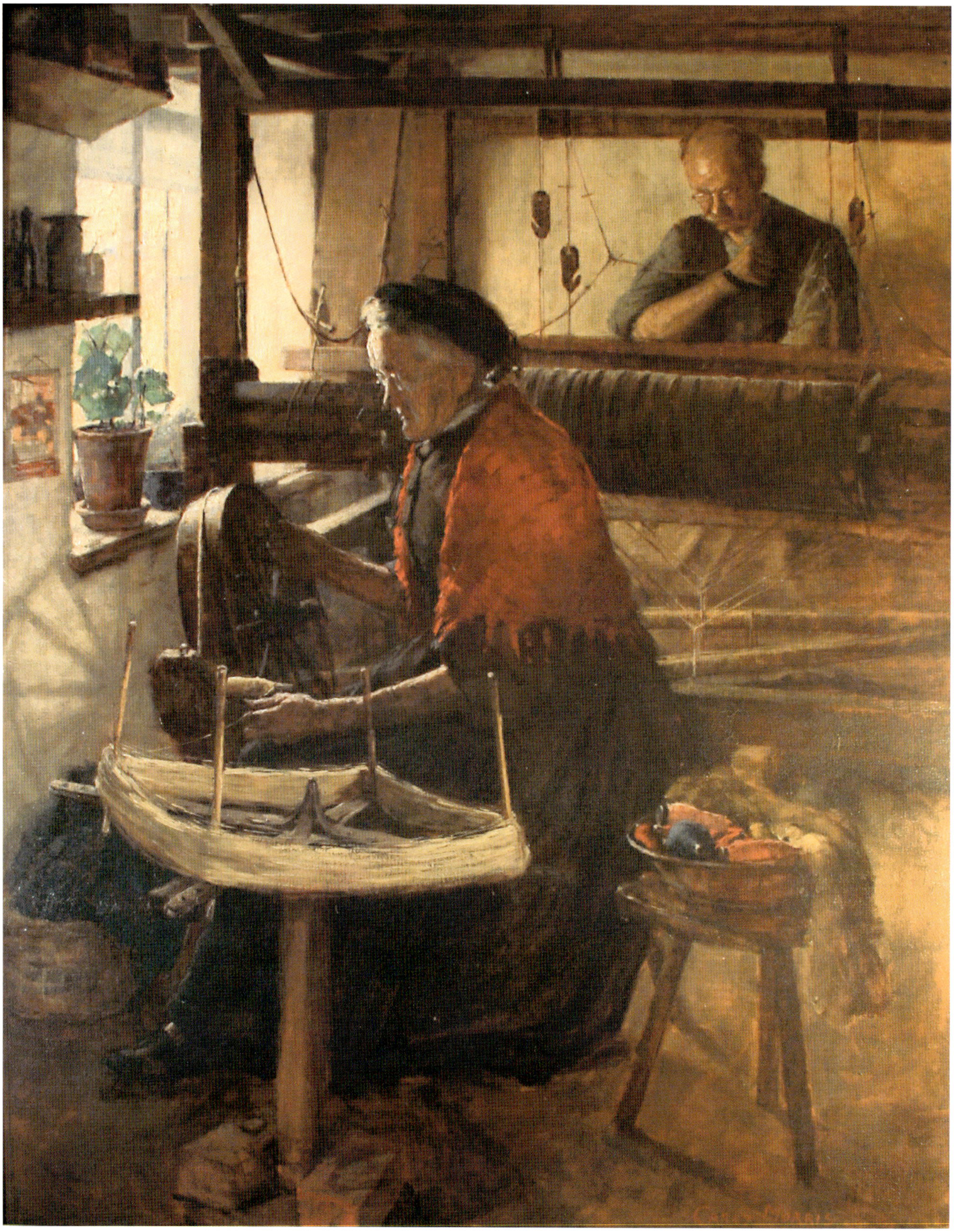

Welsh Weavers 56" x 44"

Welsh Weavers was the third painting in a series of five of his very large oil works on canvas exhibited at the Royal Academy. The abiding overall impression created by this famous oil painting, with its great human appeal, is of the immeasurable dignity of honest craftsmanship.

In 1911 Carey married his fiancée, Miss Jessie Phillips, in London. She hailed from Breconshire and was educated at two prestigious schools – the Welsh Girls' School in Ashford, Middlesex, and the North London Collegiate School for Girls, under Dr Sophie Bryant who became headmistress in 1895. Jessie Phillips embarked on a literary career and became a Fleet Street writer and journalist, and later editor of *The Young Woman*, besides editing Free Church Council publications. Jessie Phillips Morris was well-known as a short-story writer and wrote children's stories for *Blackie's Children's Annual*. She continued her literary career after her marriage. There were no children.

In 1919, describing Carey's painting *A Welsh Fisherwoman* she wrote:

> This old fisherwoman is one of a number only to be found in the quaint old-world village of Llangwm, on Milford Haven, Pembrokeshire. They are splendidly made, and have always lived on in equality with their men folk, sharing the same labours and privileges. They think nothing of fishing all day and walking thirty or forty miles next day to sell their fish. The costume is the everyday costume of the women, who obtain very picturesque effects with different coloured kerchiefs. Strangers are not warmly welcomed in this village, and this picture is the result of much persuasion and perseverance, this being the first time any Llangwm woman had consented, to sit to an artist.

The previous year she had written with anticipatory nostalgia of Carey's painting *Welsh Weavers*, in *The Cottager and Artisan*:

> Far away from the smoke of our modern factories, Mrs Edwards, the old lady shown in the painting, has for over half a century spun and woven her beautiful cloth of various hues. The wheel she handles so lovingly was used by her grandmother and great-grand-mother before her. She is over 80 years of age, but still puts in a good day's work at the spinning wheel, while her son, who is himself getting an old man now, works at the loom. They are the last of the weavers in the beautiful valley of the Tywi, and many visitors, especially from America, come to see them, and to buy their wares. Some of the Americans cast longing eyes upon the old spinning wheel, but nothing would induce the old lady to part with it. Her children would like her to put in the new-fangled machinery that turns out the cloth by the hundred yards, but she will have none of it. That cloth she says scornfully, lasts a year; the cloth made on her wheel lasts a lifetime! "They shall never put in the new machinery – not until I die," she says passionately. Thus goes on the old battle between ancients and the moderns; the old plea for leisureliness, and thoroughness; and the new craving for speed and quantity and quick profits. It is good, amid the hurry and rush and squalor of our modern industrial life, to turn aside for a moment to contemplate the life of this old lady, serenely carrying on her work amid the peaceful beauty of the Welsh hills, clinging steadfastly to the handicraft of her forefathers. Let us hope it will be a long time before "the last of the weavers" snaps the link binding the feverish present to the quiet past.

Carey and his wife shared a deep love of Wales and together saw the moon rise over Snowdon and I think Carey's elegant description demonstrates his acute perception of colours:

> It was two o'clock when we reached the margin of the snow that covered the peak of Crib Goch. So far we had climbed by the aid of the stars, but by now they had vanished leaving us in a strange weird light, through which we saw one another's faces dimly. From the opaque masses of clouds above us, a faint strip of blue emerged, merging with a lakelet of colour that paled into exquisite green, and with a still serenity and peace, the silver crescent appeared. To the right awful crags loomed darkly; beyond, Moel Siabod gleamed like one huge emerald; and in the distance, wave upon wave of rounded hills rolled into view. Far below, the track by which we had come glistened, a mere silver thread, and one by one, as the moon rays reached them, the lakes shone out like jewels. One could almost hear the rays falling through the great silence of that wondrous moonrise.

Carey's artistic description of Crib Goch and Moel Siabod in the moonlight brought him the heartfelt praise of one unrivalled in his knowledge and love of the mountains of north Wales, and whose paintings of these mountains are unsurpassed – Sir Kyffin Williams.

3 THE FRONT LINE AND AFTER

At the outbreak of war in 1914, Carey joined the Inns of Court Officer Training Corps and became Quartermaster Sergeant in the Hampshire Regiment. His friend, Brigadier-General Costello, told me something of Carey's war history.

Carey undertook officer training in Cambridge and was amused that he was allowed to use the Girton Ladies' College swimming pool. He refused a commission in the Hampshire Regiment, because his father had told him that the South Wales Borderers (SWB) was the best regiment in the army, so he was commissioned as a lieutenant into that regiment. Carey recorded some of his World War I experiences in Belgium and France. This first extract highlights his acute perception of colour and sense of history:

> As we marched on to the training ground at Rouen on a January morning a keen, icy blast blew into our faces which almost took off our noses, despite the glorious sunshine. Frozen snow lay everywhere. Gazing at this parade ground for the first time, one thought it rather strange to see soldiers in khaki marching up and down when informed that Napoleon used it for the same purpose for his intended invasion of England's shores. Now it was the training base of the British Army. On the left side of the square was a rampart where, at intervals, a French trumpeter appeared in blue and red uniform. It was like an illustrated page from the history of the Franco-German War of 1870. Extending my gaze to the other end of the square, which was some distance away, I saw a troop of Indian Lancers appear from the right-hand corner. At a sudden command they quickened their pace, then lowered their lances and charged up and down, wheeling in different directions at a tremendous pace. While I was watching this thrilling sight there appeared from the opposite corner a battery of French artillery and they, too, swept up and down at great speed. It was a wonderful sight.

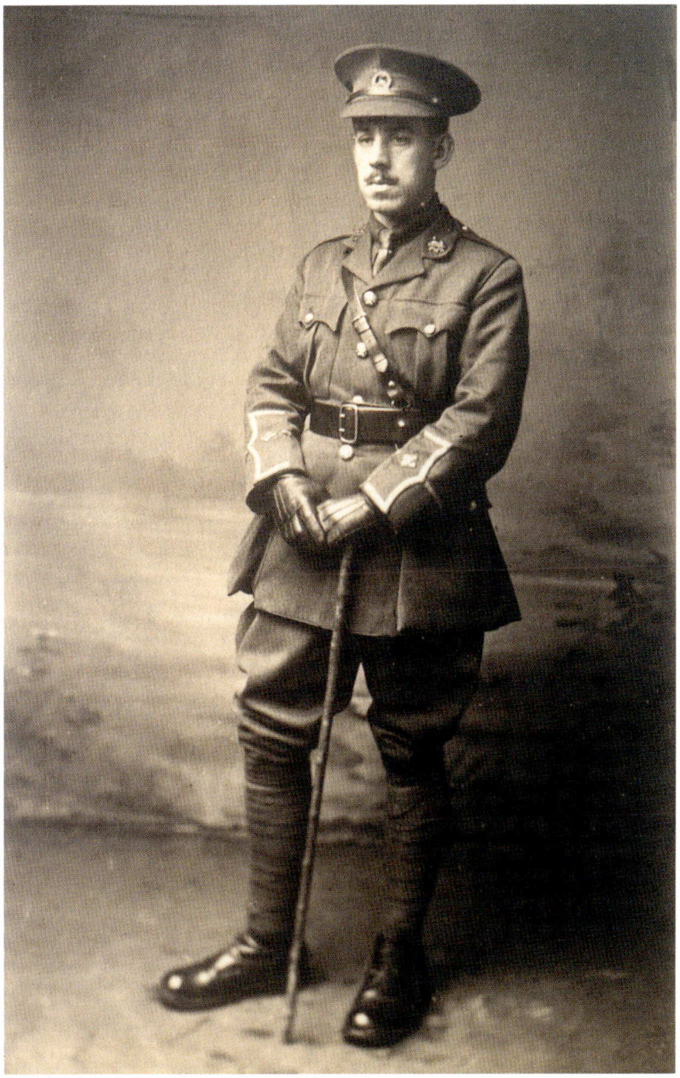

Lt Carey Morris

The colouring, fine horsemanship, discipline and control were superb. For the moment my thoughts were back home; I really thought I was at the Army and Navy Tournament in London.

Our five days' training was over, and we were now waiting orders to proceed to our respective units. I was asked by an officer of the SWB, "Where are you going?" I replied, "10th SWB." "Oh, you are going to the Ypres Salient and are for the high jump. I've just come from there, and it's hell. The time limit up there is a fortnight. You'll either be dead or a casualty in that time," he said. Cheerful news, indeed.

On Saturday afternoon we entrained in a long troop train and were quite ignorant of our destination or how long we would be on the journey. We were still on our journey in the early hours of Monday morning when an R.E. officer came into our compartment for a chat. From him we gathered that Poperinghe was our stopping-place. On approaching this town it was still dark. Our new friend directed our gaze to what appeared like fireworks (Verey lights) in the distance, and said, "The front line is yonder, and that is where you are going". [Poperinghe was in fact only about six miles from the front line at the Ypres Salient.] In the distances we could hear the booming of guns, and, with some apprehension, our friend exclaimed, "Did you hear that? There is a heavy bombardment going on. Some poor fellows are catching it in the neck."

We reached Poperinghe about eight o'clock, cramped and aching, having been on that wretched train since four p.m. on Saturday. We crossed the road to the officers' club, where we had a very welcome breakfast which we ate ravenously. Meanwhile, 'runners' had arrived to escort new officers to their units. Three of us had been posted to the 1st Gwent Battalion (10th SWB). Our runner first of all took us to our transport lines and there the quartermaster loaded us with all sorts of junk with the advice that "we would need it all up in the line". We had already walked miles, but we had about four miles to travel again on the rough road loaded with our gear.

It was on this route that Carey sketched *The Chateau at Boesinghe*, with the few tubes of paint available to him. On this road from Boesinghe to Langemark a plaque to the memory of the poet of the Black Chair of Birkenhead was erected in 1992. In Welsh, English and Flemish it records that Private Ellis Humphrey Evans (Hedd Wyn) of the 15th Battalion of the Royal Welsh Fusiliers was mortally wounded nearby on 31 July 1917. Carey recalls:

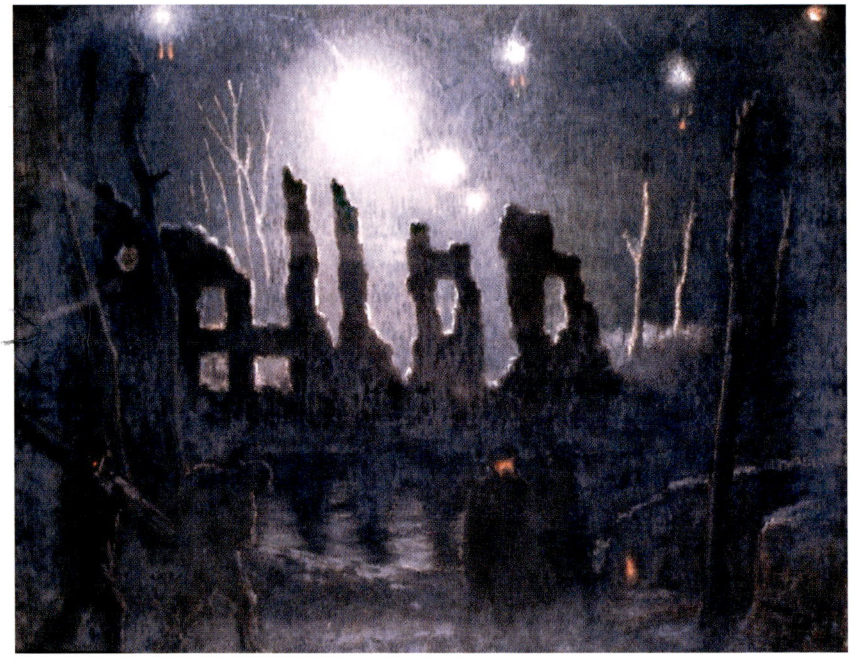

The Chateau at Boesinghe 1915 20" x 24"

> As we walked along the Boesinghe road we must have looked like Esquimaux. We passed the Chateau at Boesinghe and emerged into the village street. We had barely crossed the road when a few shells fell on the spot we had just passed. Approaching us were the commanding officer (Col. Harvey) and the adjutant (Capt. Orford). The Colonel, having noted the shells, greeted us thus: "Your luck is in already." So it was; we had had a narrow shave. We passed on to our companies. I had been posted to "A" Company and duly reported to the commander, Capt. Galsworthy, who already knew me by name. From Boesinghe we went back to Elverdinghe, and in the pagoda dug-out [a landmark known to many] I met Lt Elliot Seager, who had returned from a training course.

Carey had lost most of his tubes of paint in a bombardment after sketching the Chateau at Boesinghe. However he had managed to collect a few pieces of charcoal from the ruins surrounding him and made a sketch which he called *The Bombardment – Flanders 1917* and on the back of this sketch he wrote: 'The Bosch are using Verey lights which come down to earth like rays of gold.'

To be able even to think of painting and drawing in such circumstances surely illustrates his overwhelming passion for art. After making the short journey back to the dug-out at Elverdinghe, Carey was sent back to the horrors of the front line via the Pilckem Ridge.

> We returned again to the front line, this time across the canal, at the foot of Pilkem [sic] Ridge. Now permit me to give you a momentary glimpse into the abyss. It was late in the evening and I had just been relieved by Lt Elliot Seager and prepared to have a few hours' rest in the dug-out (a hole in the ground).

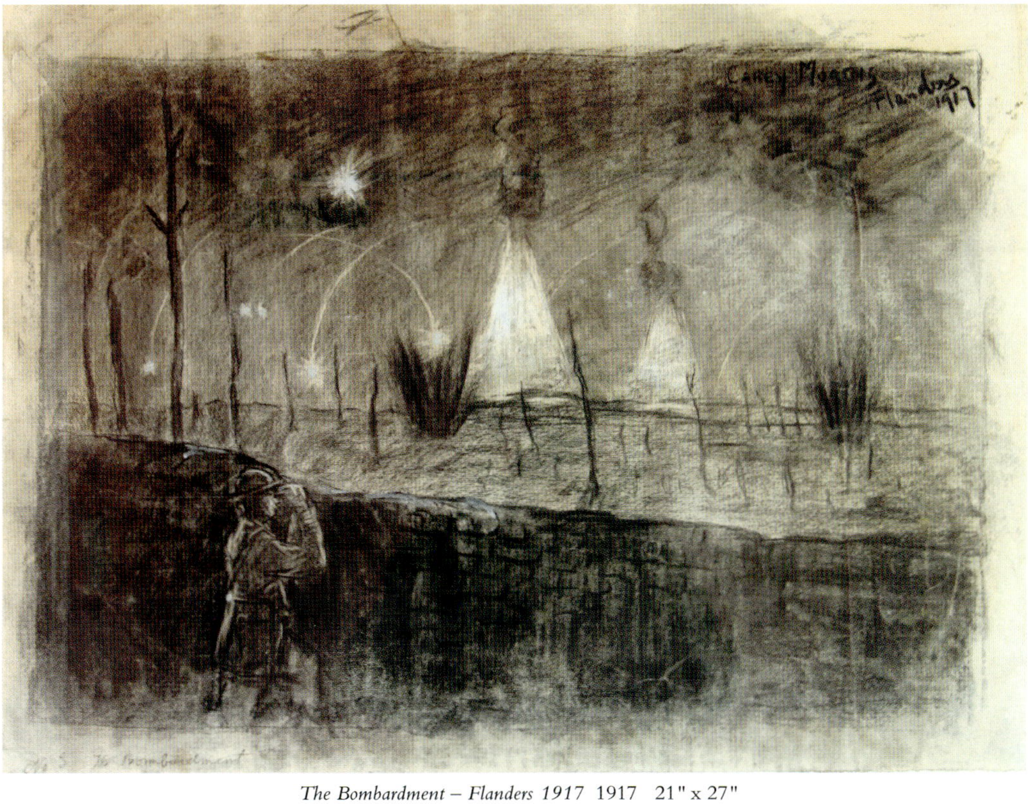

The Bombardment – Flanders 1917 1917 21" x 27"

> Hardly had I turned in when I heard the rattle of machine guns. I felt at once that all was not well, so hurriedly I got my things together when the order "Stand to everybody" came to my ears. I rushed up to the front line and found that once there it was impossible to get away on account of the heavy bombardment.

Then Carey, uncharacteristically, lets us have a graphically gruesome description of what it was really like on the front line:

> Everything on both sides was being hurled over. Heavy shells, shrapnel, machine gun and rifle fire, and trench mortars. It was hell let loose. We were all on the firestep peering into the gloom, ready for any sudden attack. Above the din I heard a terrific explosion very near; there was a tremendous rattle of metal in front of me, and at that moment a soft wet mass struck me in the face and on the chest. I felt faint for the moment and, when I removed the mass off my face with my hand, I realised with sadness in my heart that it was the flesh of one of our own men. We called the roll as soon as the 'strafe' was over and found that we had lost six men, four of whom had been blown to pieces. Some of these pieces had reached me 20 yards away. The intense bombardment lasted five hours, but this sort of thing was a daily occurrence. This one incident should be enough to deter anyone from rushing headlong into a war again.

I believe that Carey described this nauseating experience, one of many, to bring us face to face with the loathsome behemoth that is war. Then, as though in an attempt to bring us back to normality, he relates a humorous episode:

> About this time I went to the Divisional School near Proven and, on the last day of the course, I visited Poperinghe to make a few purchases before returning to the front line. While waiting in the shop, which had an estaminet attached, an officer came up to the counter and, addressing the young woman who served me, said, "Juliette, I am returning to the front, and I may never see you again. I want to buy you something before I go. What will you have?" After a mild sort of protestation Juliette replied, "I'll have a box of chocolates, monsieur". She selected a large box from a glass case on the counter, and handed it to the officer who presented it back with the 14 francs, the price of the box. As soon as the officer had gone, she replaced the box back in the glass case. Presently, another officer came out from the estaminet, and walked up to the counter. He, too, wished to make a present to Juliette much in the same manner as the previous officer. The young woman went through the same procedure, and when the second officer had departed the same box was again placed back in the glass case. If this ceremony went on every day that box of chocolates must have brought in a small fortune to her. I left the shop much amused and started on my long tramp to the front line to rejoin my unit.

Carey returned to the front line at Brieleu where he had a providential escape from being blown into shreds, as he recounts:

> When I arrived at Brieleu I had already walked about seven miles on a rough cobbled road, and my heels

> were quite sore. It was past midnight, and I felt very thirsty. There wasn't a soul to be seen anywhere. I didn't expect to see civilians, as there were none, the village having been reduced to ruins. At last I espied a chink of light in one of the houses. I turned in there and found a young artillery officer writing. He made me welcome and supplied me with some hot tea. I stayed with him for some time, as I had walked about twelve miles since three o'clock in the afternoon and needed rest. Eventually I took my departure and soon rejoined my company on the other side of the canal bank. Directly afterwards Capt. Galsworthy had to visit Brieleu, but returned quite soon. He told me that as he entered Brieleu he heard the scream of a shell which fell into one of the houses in the street and into a room where a battery major and a young artillery officer were sitting, killing both outright. For a few moments I could hardly speak. Then I told him that I had been resting for a few hours in that very room, chatting with the young officer, now dead, on my way back. Our company was still in the front line, but was about to be relieved by "B" Company.

Before leaving the trenches Carey used his bits of charcoal to make another sketch which he called *The Billet – Flanders 1917*. 'After a gruelling time in the line we were quite glad to get away from it for a while and, as we marched out, a runner came up to me with a chit. To my annoyance, it informed me that I would be staying behind to continue another five days in the line with "B" Company.'

Carey then voices his opinion on the inanity of some of the very high-ranking officers who remained well behind the front line:

> The following day I was detailed to take a patrol out into "No Man's Land" between eleven and twelve o'clock at night. The terrain was bathed in brilliant moonlight, and the absurdity of sending us out on such a night struck me forcibly. Considering the "stalemate" position of the war at the time, these patrols served very little purpose except, perhaps, to enable senior officers in the rear to get decorations. The infantry were often puzzled at the action of the War Office in sending cavalry officers with little or no knowledge of infantry work to take charge of

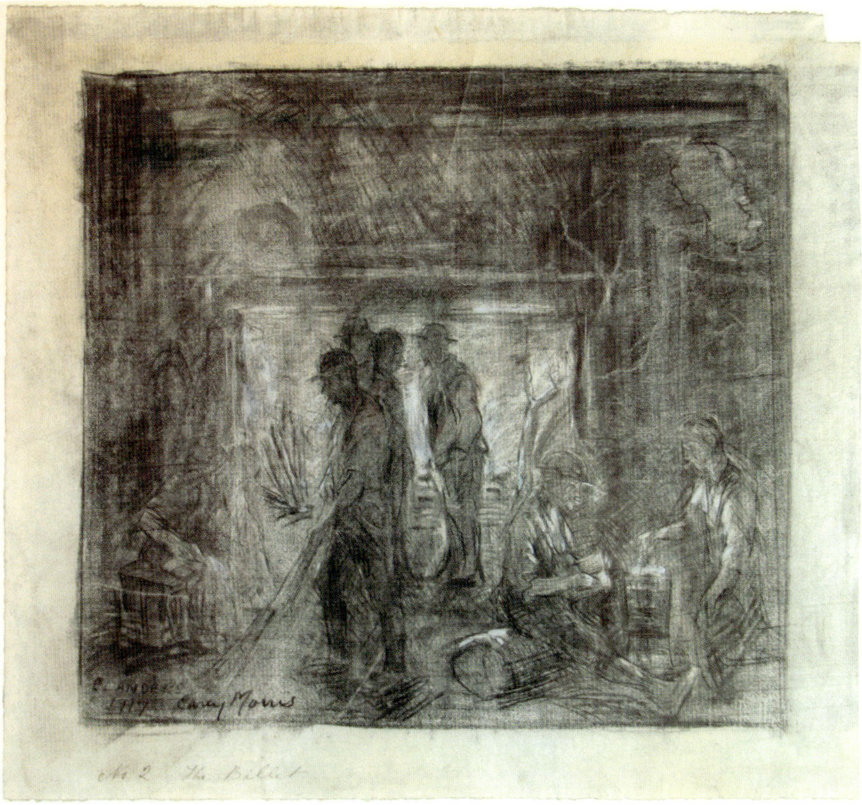

The Billet – Flanders 1917 1917 21" x 23"

infantry brigades and battalions in trench warfare. The general opinion was that we would have got on better if half the 'Brass Hats' had been sent home with a rattle in their hands. So many lacked inventiveness and imagination and the requirements of modern warfare were quite beyond some of them.

He then continues and gives a further illustration of the lack of imagination and intelligence of some of the 'brass hats':

I heard the following story while on the staff of the Camouflage School in London in 1918. It was told by a highly-placed official who was visiting the school at the time. Some guns had been placed in position in a chalk quarry at the rear of the front line in France. One of the battery officers approaching the quarry from his dug-out noticed the brightness of the polished metal parts of the guns glistening in the sunlight. He had the sense to order his men to plaster chalk all over the metal parts in order to dull them so that they would be less discernible to the enemy. Unfortunately for him, a "Brass Hat" came along and noticed the chalk on the guns. The officer was severely reprimanded by the "Brass Hat" for not keeping his guns clean and smart. More than that, he was court-martialled as well. At the time, the art of camouflage was receiving some attention, as it was learnt that the Germans were making great use of it. News of the incident reached the ears of the highly-placed official, who immediately went over to France to investigate. The unimaginative "Brass Hat" was sent home and the artillery officer was complimented.

Carey left the front line to prepare for a concerted thrust on the German front line. Even in these ominous circumstances, his sense of fun, never far beneath the surface, bubbles up and he tells an amusing tale:

Early in July 1917, our division had been relieved by the Guards. We were now preparing to leave the Boesinghe sector for some unknown destination presumably a training ground – and to prepare for some big offensive.

One afternoon I was sent to Poperinghe to find billets for the officers of the battalion. The colonel should have sent me in the morning, for when I arrived in the town the other battalions had stolen a march on us and had booked nearly all the billets. However, I managed to get two billets at the officers' club, and these I reserved for the colonel and adjutant. I was informed at the club that perhaps I would be able to find billets for the remaining officers at the convent in the next street. I went there and interviewed the Mother Superior, who took me up a staircase and showed me a number of cubicles which we could have, but that it would be necessary for me to see the Town Mayor first of all to obtain his approval. Having visited the latter, I returned to the convent and told the Mother Superior we would be arriving about midnight. It was very dark when we arrived. I led the officers to the convent, but in darkness I was quite at a loss to direct the officers to the cubicles I had seen in daylight. Capt. Galsworthy and I went up a staircase which I imagined was the one I had been up in the day, but when we heard women coughing we discovered that we were in the nuns' quarters, and on the wrong staircase and hastily retreated. Meanwhile the other officers had found the cubicles. By this time it was hardly worth while turning in as we had to parade again at four o'clock.

After this interlude, Carey marched his men via Proven to Hazebrouck where, even under stress, his artistic temperament and love of Wales shone through:

It was market day at this place, and how I longed to stay in that Square to paint pictures of the market place and the quaint people about. It seemed strange that I was doing something quite the opposite. As we tramped away the quick impressions I had of the market square still linger in my memory. We arrived at Laires, not far from Lillers. The country here reminded me of Wales, most of the farms being lime-washed.

Again, Carey's love of life becomes apparent, but in this extract it is tempered by his taste, on occasions, for a little black humour:

We remained at Laires for a few weeks. Our company officers' mess was in the house of a carpenter, wheelwright, undertaker, and farmer rolled in one. One morning, while I was having my breakfast, the landlord asked whether there was an artist in the company. Capt. Galsworthy turned to me and said, "Here's a commission for you, old boy". I asked the landlord what he wanted, and he informed me that he had a coffin to make for a great sportsman in the village and that the gentleman had expressed a desire to have a picture of a hare sitting on its haunches with landscape painted as large as possible on the coffin lid. I said that I would do it with pleasure if I could find some paints and brushes I had somewhere in my valise. I eventually found them but I was a bit stumped for a hare as a model. The landlord then took me to the back yard and showed some rabbits in hutches. I made a rough sketch of one of the rabbits and turned it into a hare by drawing the ears and the hind legs larger. My range of colours was limited as I had lost some tubes of paint while attempting to sketch in Boesinghe village, which was too dangerous a job as the shells were continually dropping in the street.

However Carey had succeeded in sketching the Chateau at Boesinghe:

I managed to get some ordinary house paint from the carpenter, and having got all my materials together I proceeded with my work of art. The news that an artist was painting a picture on the lid of a coffin spread like wildfire through the village and shortly there was a crowd outside pressing hard against the window and endeavouring to catch a glimpse at the artist working on such a gruesome and unusual canvas. I managed to get a fairly good representation of a hare which looked quite effective against a big sky and trees. When it was complete the carpenter invited the villagers to view the work of art. It was like a one-man art exhibition. Slowly the villagers left the room, but one old man lingered on, and when he was about to leave I asked the carpenter, "When is the owner of the coffin to be buried?" "He isn't dead yet. There he is going out now," said he, pointing to the old man leaving the house. "Yes, he is a great sportsman. I do not remember the number of times he has been in prison for poaching," added the carpenter.

When the training was over we began our long march back to the Salient. By this time a serious illness came upon me and I left the battalion at Proven and returned to "Blighty", where I spent the next twelve months in different hospitals and in this way missed the great offensive of July 30, 1917. A few weeks later Company-Sergeant-Major Jack Williams of "B" Company won the Victoria Cross for great gallantry.

★ ★ ★ ★

In 1918, at the end of his convalescence, aged 36, determined to pursue his artistic career despite ill health, he enrolled at the Slade School of Art in London for refresher courses in drawing and painting. His tutor was the great artist, Sir Alfred Munnings, later President of the Royal Academy, and he had a very high opinion of Carey's work, as did the Slade Professor of Fine Art, Henry Tonks, the eminent surgeon who gave up medicine to teach drawing at the Slade, but who returned to medicine as a plastic surgeon in World War I.

It was Carey's detailed knowledge of the relation between the contours of the body and the underlying bone and muscle, gained from his study of *Gray's Anatomy* as a teenager, that gave his portraits their uncanny three-dimensional qualities and so impressed Professor Tonks, as exemplified in his study *A Slade Model* and *The Connoisseur.*

In his account Carey had, in fact, omitted to mention an important turn of events which was later revealed by Brigadier-General Costello. It appears that while acting as second in command of his company, Carey was detailed to make a plan of

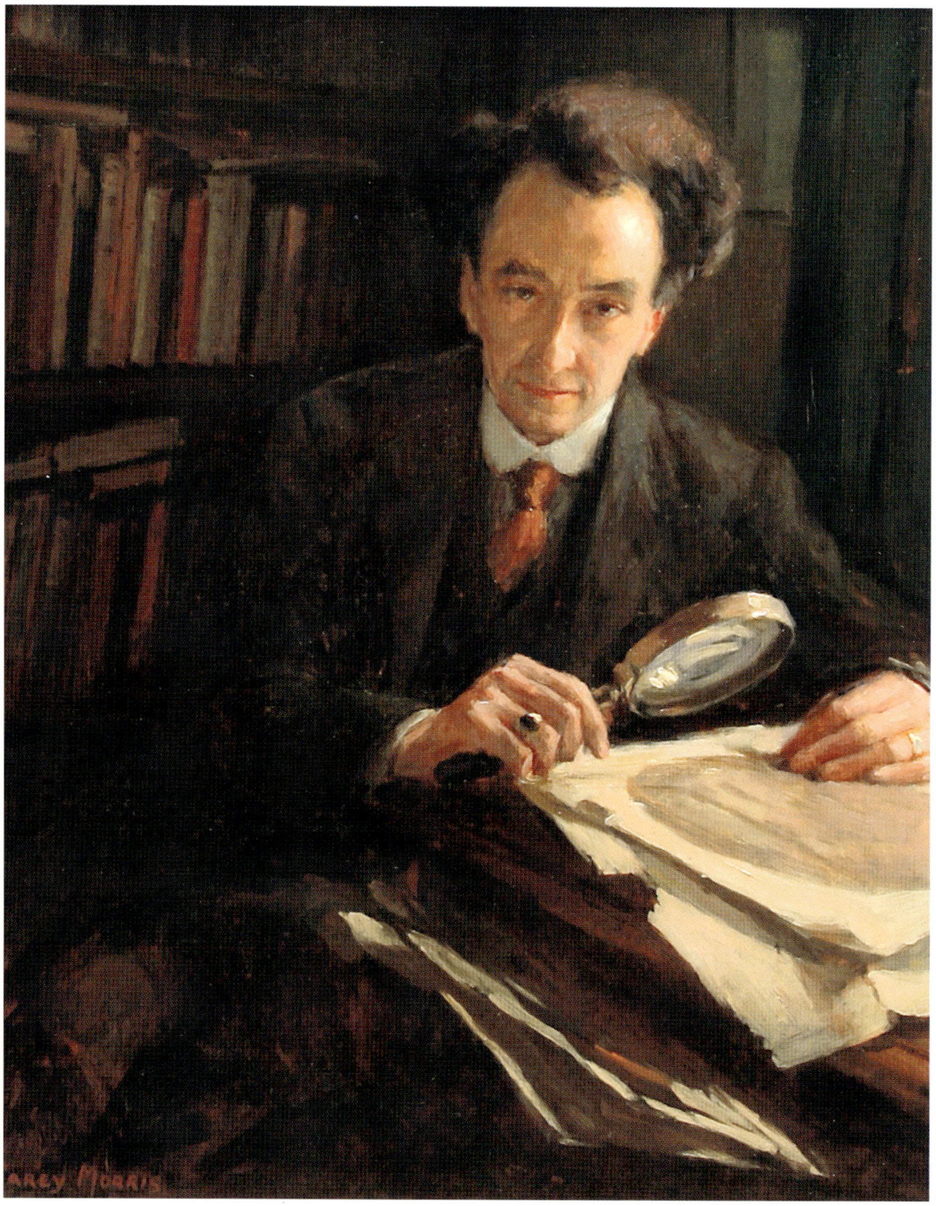

The Connoisseur 1920 19½" x 15½"

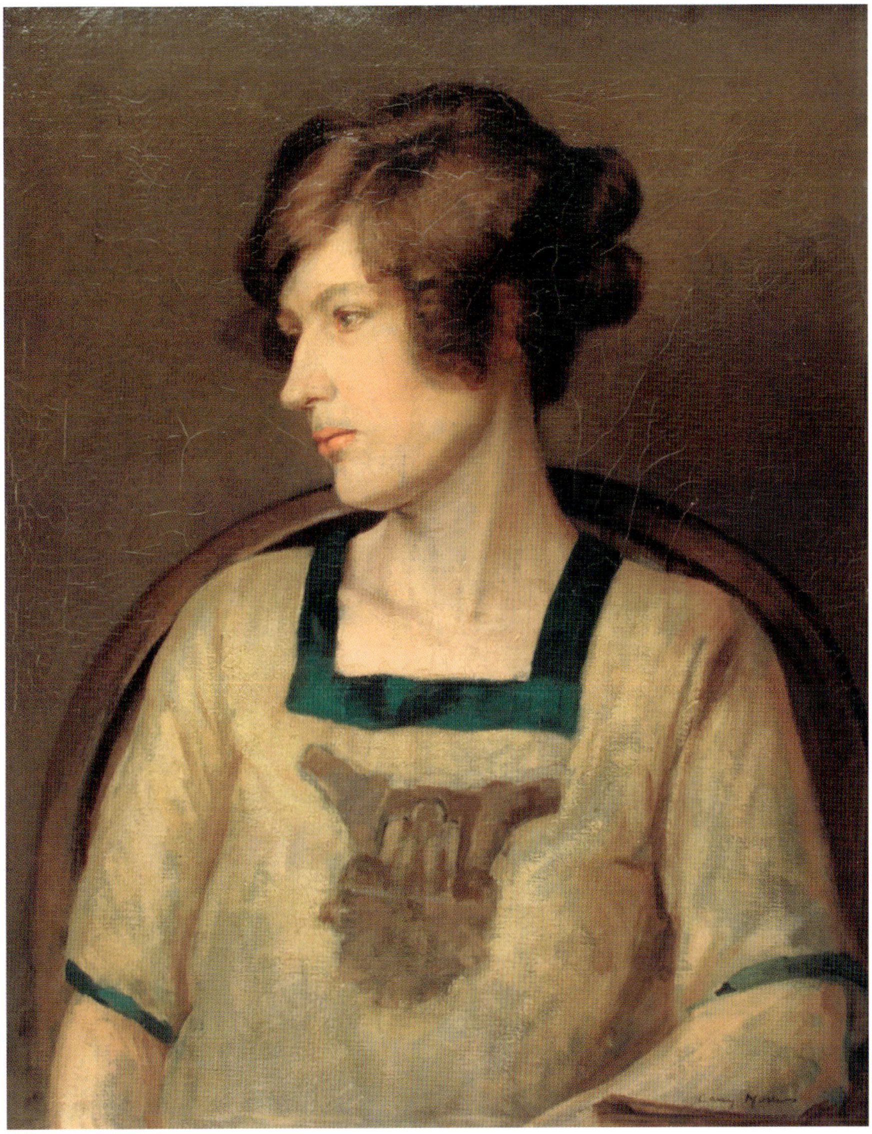

A Slade Model 1919 23½" x 17½"

the trench system. The plan was passed up to the General, who was so impressed that Carey was forthwith promoted to a Major in the Intelligence Corps. But it was at this juncture that the serious illness he refers to occurred. It was, in fact, due to the poison chlorine gas, first used by the Germans, near Pilckem Ridge and Ypres Salient, in flagrant disregard of international law. This cowardly and atrocious act of the Germans against Allied troops caused untold misery and blindness, while thousands died horrible deaths, gasping for breath, staggering about in wild panic with grey faces and purple lips, spitting blood in the choking green mist that enveloped them. As Wilfred Owen wrote in his war poem, 'Dulce et Decorum Est':

> Dim through the misty panes and thick green light,
> As under a green sea, I saw him drowning.
> In all my dreams, before my helpless sight,
> He plunges at me, guttering, choking, drowning.

If it does not kill, inhalation of chlorine gas destroys lung tissue leaving permanent scarring of the lungs, and often leaving psychological damage, too. On being invalided back to Britain, Carey spent a year in hospital. On his discharge the war was over and, before going to the Slade, he spent some months convalescing with his brother who was a vicar at Pennard on the Gower peninsula where, in an attempt to become fit again, he went swimming every morning. Though Carey suffered permanent lung damage, for which he received a miserably inadequate war disability pension, he certainly never betrayed any psychological harm. On the contrary, he was always cheerful and happy and nothing could dampen his effervescent sense of humour.

He was to die 50 years later, but his friends still remembered him, and a red poppy appeared on his grave on Remembrance Day.

4 THE EISTEDDFOD

In 1922 the Royal National Eisteddfod of Wales made a wise decision. It appointed Carey Morris as the first Honorary Director of its Arts and Crafts section. He devoted so much time and energy to the work and achieved such wonderful results that he was re-elected time and again as Honorary Director during the 1920s. As a consequence the Arts and Crafts section became one of the most successful parts of the Eisteddfod.

As a professional artist trained at Newlyn and the Slade, he was able to influence artists of calibre and attract them to the Arts and Crafts section as exhibitors and adjudicators and so raise the level of the competitions. This happy state of affairs obtained throughout the years he was director. Great artists such as Augustus John, Sir Frank Brangwyn, John Sargent, Sir John Lavery, Walter Sickert, Sir Max Beerbohm, Evan Walters, Sir William Orpen, Christopher Williams, Sir George Clausen, John Nash, Sir William Goscombe-John, as well as Claude Monet, were happy to exhibit their works at the Eisteddfod and many of them also acted as adjudicators. The work of great artists of the past such as Richard Wilson, J.D. Innes, Gainsborough, Constable, J.M.W. Turner, Corot, Manet, Gauguin, Rossetti, Sir Edward Poynter, Sir Edward Burne-Jones, David Cox, Lord Leighton and van Dyck were exhibited. It was the golden era of Arts and Crafts in the Eisteddfod, and all under the guidance of Carey Morris.

In those days Prime Ministers such as David Lloyd George, Ramsay MacDonald and even Stanley Baldwin presided at the Eisteddfod, and the President of the Royal Academy, Sir Francis Dicksee, opened the Arts and Crafts exhibition. In fact, the standards in the Arts and Crafts competitions were so high that Lloyd George predicted that: 'If these standards were maintained, then Wales would establish the same enviable position in the art world as she had already achieved in the world of music.' He went on to say: 'The Eisteddfod is 40 years older than Magna Carta and, if one speaks of the House of Commons as being the Mother of Parliaments, then the Eisteddfod is old enough to be its Grandmother!' He was, of course, referring to the earliest Eisteddfod for which there are full written records, which was held at Cardigan Castle in 1176 under the patronage of the Lord Rhys, though it is believed that Owain, son of Magnus Maximus, had already brought order to the meetings of bards as early as 375AD.

Carey and his associates persuaded Mrs Winifred Coombe Tennant, the foremost patron of Welsh art in the twentieth century, to lend paintings from her collection for the Arts and Crafts exhibitions. Carey, together with Isaac Williams, Keeper of Art in the National Museum, managed to induce the Davies sisters of Gregynog to lend works by the French Impressionist Monet, the Post-Impressionist Gauguin and the landscape artist, Corot. The National Museum in Cardiff lent paintings by Richard Wilson; the Victoria and Albert Museum, Lord Howard de Walden and the Tate Gallery also lent works.

Carey pioneered the educational aspects of the Arts and Crafts exhibitions and encouraged schools to send their pupils to visit, and be taken on specially arranged guided tours and join in discussions about the art works on display. This innovative idea resulted in many hundreds of school children visiting the arts exhibitions.

To Carey the term 'Art' did not only refer to the higher non-utilitarian fine arts of painting and sculpture, but also embraced poetry, music and drama, as evidenced in his article, 'Art and the Drama' in *Y Cerddor Newydd*, May 1924. He wrote: 'At the Royal National Eisteddfod of Wales at Pontypool this year, one of the special features of the Art Exhibition will be the Drama Section. Two rooms will be devoted to the artistic side of the drama; one will contain lighted miniature stage scenes; the other, colour and costume designs.'

He maintained that in staging a drama, though everyone recognized the work of the dramatists and actors, few appreciated the part played by artists in the design, colouring and positioning of the scenery and lighting, as well as the clothing and artistic grouping of the actors, though he did not go as far as the theatre set-designer, Edward Gordon Craig, who considered that theatre-goers were more interested in seeing rather than hearing the performance. He continues:

> Lord Howard de Walden and Joseph Holbrooke are lending us a number of Sime's designs for their Welsh operas. Rutland Boughton is arranging for us to have some of the original designs for his Celtic opera *The Immortal Hour*, and also *Alkestis*; the Birmingham Repertory Theatre are lending designs for the same composer's *Bethlehem*. The Drama rooms will therefore appeal to all those interested in Painting, Music and Literature, as it is connected with all three arts. The chief quality that our Welsh dramatists must strive to cultivate is artistic taste… There is no difference in the process that goes on in the mind of the artist, whether he be painter, sculptor, musician, dramatist or poet.

Carey concludes by exhorting budding young dramatists and musicians to study the works of the great painters and to follow the example of his friend, the famous composer Rutland Boughton. He writes:

> In a talk I had recently with Rutland Boughton, who is now achieving great success, he told me he is an assiduous student of the works of the great painters, and that while he composed much in Wales and drew inspiration from the Welsh Hills, he also found inspiration for the design and patterns of his music in works of Art. I commend his example both to our young musicians and dramatists. Let them drink deep from the fount of inspiration in the Land of their Fathers, the folklore and music, and the beautiful natural scenery; but let them also not neglect to study great works of art, in whatever country or whatever guise they may be found. Let them bring the artistic knowledge and taste thus acquired into the fashioning of their own native works. By following this method of going both to Life and to Art for their inspiration, they will produce a native drama true to Life, but lifted out of its present crudity by the artistic skill of the dramatist.

Carey, ever-mindful of the necessity of maintaining and enhancing the dignity of the Gorsedd proceedings, which represent one of our few remaining time-honoured and colourful national ceremonial occasions, eventually succeeded in persuading the authorities to replace the blaring cacophony of the brass bands with the elegant notes of just two silver trumpets as preamble to the ceremonies. He would be delighted too that, at last, the druids and bards in their robes do not now have to be ferried around in a fleet of double-decker buses, but now robe in rooms at the back of the main pavilion, as he had recommended as far back as the 1920s.

Carey was very cognisant of the fact that aspiring artists were obliged to leave Wales to be trained and, as a result, he persuaded a fellow professional artist, Tim Evans, to join him in campaigning for the founding of a truly national school of art for Wales. The idea was to start art classes in drawing, watercolour, pastel and oil for landscapes and portraits. The classes would be held at various locations around Wales in the hope that the venture would stimulate a widespread interest in the visual arts and lead to the creation of a definitive Welsh school of art.

Carey and his associates, supported by other professional artists, exhibitors and adjudicators, including the sculptor Sir William Goscombe-John, continued to prevail upon the Eisteddfod authorities to appoint a permanent committee of people who *really* understood fine art, with the task of assessing the relative merits of works submitted for the competitions in an attempt to maintain the high standard that had, by now, been achieved. This committee would also advise on the best policy procedures in obtaining loans of pictures by well-known artists to continue the precedent established by Carey during the 1920s. The *Western Mail* reported on 13 August 1928 after the National Eisteddfod at Treorci: 'Mr Carey Morris who

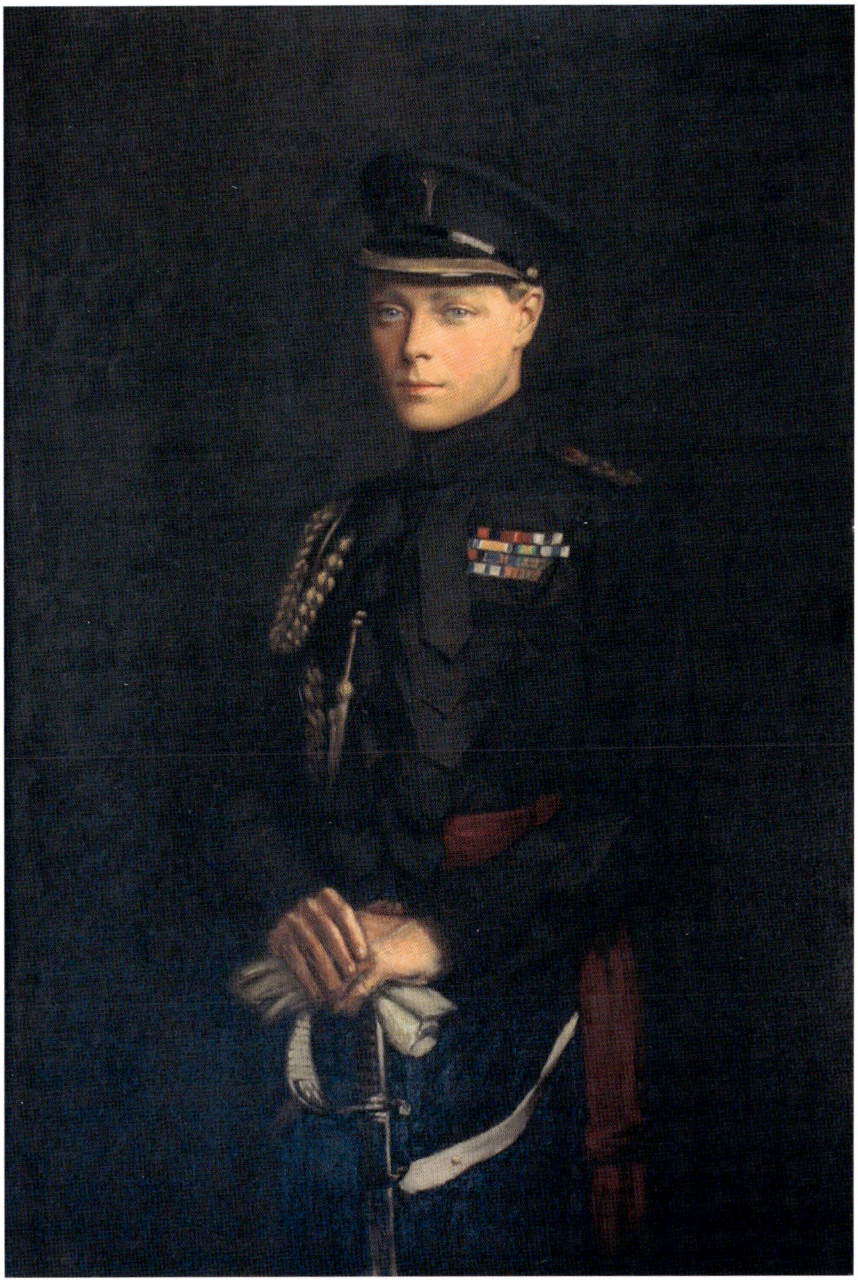

HRH The Prince of Wales 1924 54" x 35"

has sacrificed so much time and voluntary effort on behalf of the "National" also advocated drastic reforms in the organisation of the arts, crafts and science section of the Eisteddfod.' Carey's proposed committee of Welsh artists 'would function solely in an advisory capacity as far as the National Eisteddfod is concerned. While in no way assuming control, they would be available year after year to advise in questions relating to fine arts and to see that a consistent policy was maintained.'

But all to no avail the amateur art committees composed of local well-meaning people in the various areas visited by the Eisteddfod each year continued unchanged. Following the 1920s, when the Arts and Crafts section reached its golden zenith under Carey's management, there followed a rapid decline in its status and appeal. Established artists were rarely invited to exhibit, while the standard of competitions descended to the parochial level of a village show, with nothing 'national' about them. A decade of voluntary hard work by Carey and his colleagues in raising standards had been undone. This was very disheartening for Carey, but he would have been glad to know that nowadays his recommendations have, to some extent, been implemented.

For the 1924 Eisteddfod at Pontypool, Carey made an oil painting of the *Prince of Wales* (later King Edward VIII, and afterwards Duke of Windsor) at St James' Palace in his uniform as Colonel of the Welsh Guards and, with the prince's permission, the portrait was exhibited to much acclaim. Another exhibit which attracted much enthusiastic attention at the same Eisteddfod was a portable folding

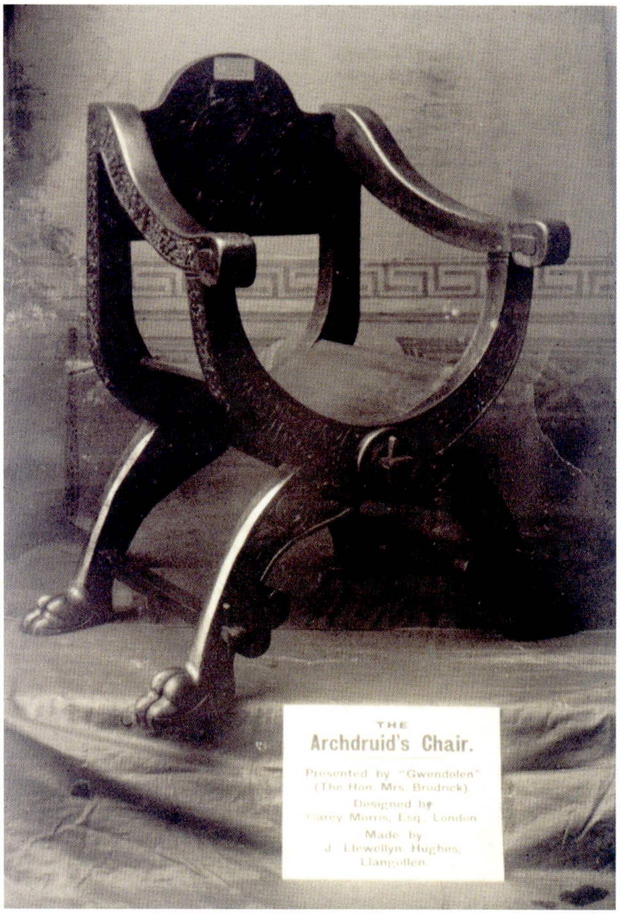

Archdruid's chair

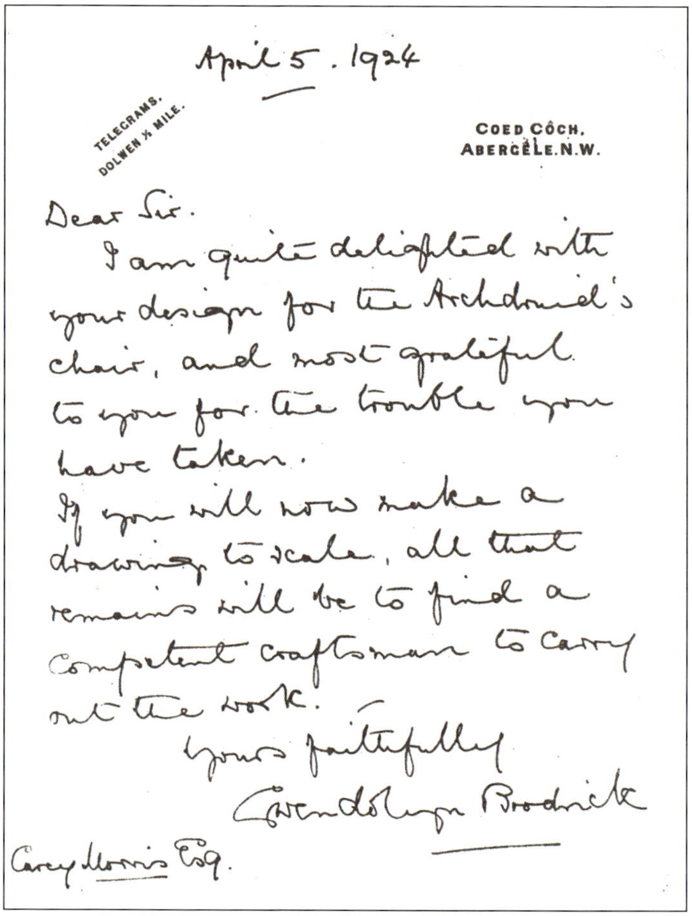

April 5. 1924

TELEGRAMS. DOLWEN ¼ MILE.

COED CÔCH.
ABERGELE. N.W.

Dear Sir.

I am quite delighted with your design for the Archdruid's chair, and most grateful to you for the trouble you have taken.

If you will now make a drawing to scale, all that remains will be to find a competent craftsman to carry out the work.

Yours faithfully
Gwendolyn Brodrick

Carey Morris Esq.

Letter from the Hon. Gwendolyn Brodrick

archdruid's chair designed by Carey, sponsored by the Hon. Gwendolyn Brodrick granddaughter of the Earl of Ravensworth, and constructed by J. Llewelyn Hughes, Llangollen.

In 1924, in view of his standing as a professional artist as well as his brilliance in fulfilling his role as Honorary Director of the Arts and Crafts section, Carey was invited by the Council of the Eisteddfod to address the Honourable Society of Cymmrodorion on the subject, 'The Teaching of Art in Wales'. He started by saying: 'Some people consider the Teaching of Art a luxury, and quite unnecessary as an item in the list of School subjects. They imagine Art to be something that begins and ends with a picture on the wall. Nothing could be further from the truth.'

He noted that the Board of Education had laid a 'cold dead hand' upon the teaching of art by giving financial grants only to art schools that employed teachers with certificates. He continued: 'To qualify for these "certificates", the aspiring artists have to be compressed down to one dead level; originality and individuality are at a discount, and the artistic personality, which is the greatest factor in Art, has to be suppressed', because to obtain a certificate one had to, 'qualify in the whole gamut of Art – drawing, painting, modelling, sculpture, etching, engraving, architecture, designing and metal work – each branch a lifetime study in itself so the Board only recognises a Jack-of-all trades'.

He pointed out that the greatest British artists at that time, such as Augustus John and Sir Frank Brangwyn, were not qualified to teach in schools, because they had not trained in the only school recognised by the Board of Education, namely the Royal College of Art, South Kensington, but rather had trained in great, but unrecognized schools such as the Slade, the Newlyn School, the Glasgow School or the Academy schools. 'So the Board of Education is nothing but a commercial trades union, whose object is to keep out, not the blackleg, but the real artist.'

To underline the absurdity of the attitude of the Board of Education, Carey then mentioned a few of the great artists teaching at schools not recognised by the Board of Education: Sir Alfred Munnings, Stanhope Forbes, Wilson Stear, Augustus John, Henry Tonks and Sir Hubert von Herkomer. He added: 'Can you wonder that it is to these unrecognized schools we look for the coming artists?' Carey states that he and other Welsh artists had to leave Wales, 'because the only art training we could obtain in Wales was that given by the Board of Education, which would be fatal to our artistic development'. Few of the artists who had to leave Wales to train came back to Wales. But, all honour to him, Carey did.

Carey received plaudits from the other speakers who shared the platform with him, and who spoke in much the same vein. Sir Daniel Lleufer Thomas, social reformer, born in Talyllychau, near Llandeilo, said:

> The too prevalent view, even among educationalists, is that art is a sort of educational "extra"... The teaching of Art should embrace professional training for the aspiring artist, practical training in drawing and the teaching of art appreciation, and this may sometimes result in an artist creating a work of beauty... It is for want of this kind of teaching in our teachers' training colleges and University that much of the Art teaching in schools is often mechanical and lifeless.

Even nowadays, nearly a century later, drawing is taught in only a few Art schools. Isaac

Williams, Carey's loyal associate, considered that: 'Any educational body that does not give efficient instruction in aesthetics is dead to the meaning of Art. The teaching of Art should cater for those with a natural gift of artistic expression, and also for those who wish to cultivate a dormant gift of art appreciation... Young Wales is largely ignorant of the existence of a native Art tradition.'

This may have been because of the lack of literature on Welsh artists, such as, Inigo Jones and Richard Wilson. This shortcoming has now been corrected by the authoritative works from Wales' foremost art historian, Peter Lord, but in those far-off days, loan collections from the National Museum of Wales in Cardiff to schools in the nearby densely populated areas of south Wales provided the only means of filling the gap, and that to a very limited extent.

Sir William Goscombe-John wrote that: 'In Wales, Art should be made an essential part of the ordinary curriculum of our Schools and Colleges.' However, missionary efforts were required 'To enlighten some of our educational authorities, who, in Art matters, seem to live in the backwoods... It has been truly said that "a love of beauty is equivalent to the possession of another sense".'

Sir Clough Williams-Ellis posed the question, 'What is Art?' and his answer was, 'I suppose it is the creation of Beauty... Educate enough and in the right way and we shall soon find that Michael Angelo has routed Napoleon as a hero from our schools and playgrounds'.

Sir Mortimer Wheeler, Director of the National Museum of Wales, emphasised, as Augustus John often did, the hopeless degradation bred by industrialism, but which could be alleviated to some extent by the chance to see and appreciate *true* art. To achieve this, there have to be teachers in our schools, where, with few exceptions, 'Art' is not interpreted as: '...the drawing of plaster pyramids. There is no reason, save that of a present deficiency of suitable teachers, why the senior classes in every secondary school at least, should not devote one or two hours a week to the discussion of reproductions of works of art.'

He made a plea for painting to be brought within the reach of the industrial population by taking advantage of the scheme of loan-collections from the art department of the National Museum of Wales, and by the adequate teaching of appreciation of art. He also mentioned, as did Carey, that: 'There is no Welsh School of Art which can approach comparison with those of London or Glasgow, or even with small schools such as Newlyn.' He deplored the fact that we accept bad art and are degraded by it, echoing not only Carey's sentiments, but also those of the greatest artist of the twentieth century in Wales, Sir Kyffin Williams.

Carey has never been credited with the recognition due to him for his invaluable pioneering work in the 1920s, often against strong opposition, in making the Arts and Crafts section of the National Eisteddfod of Wales reach its all-time pinnacle of excellence.

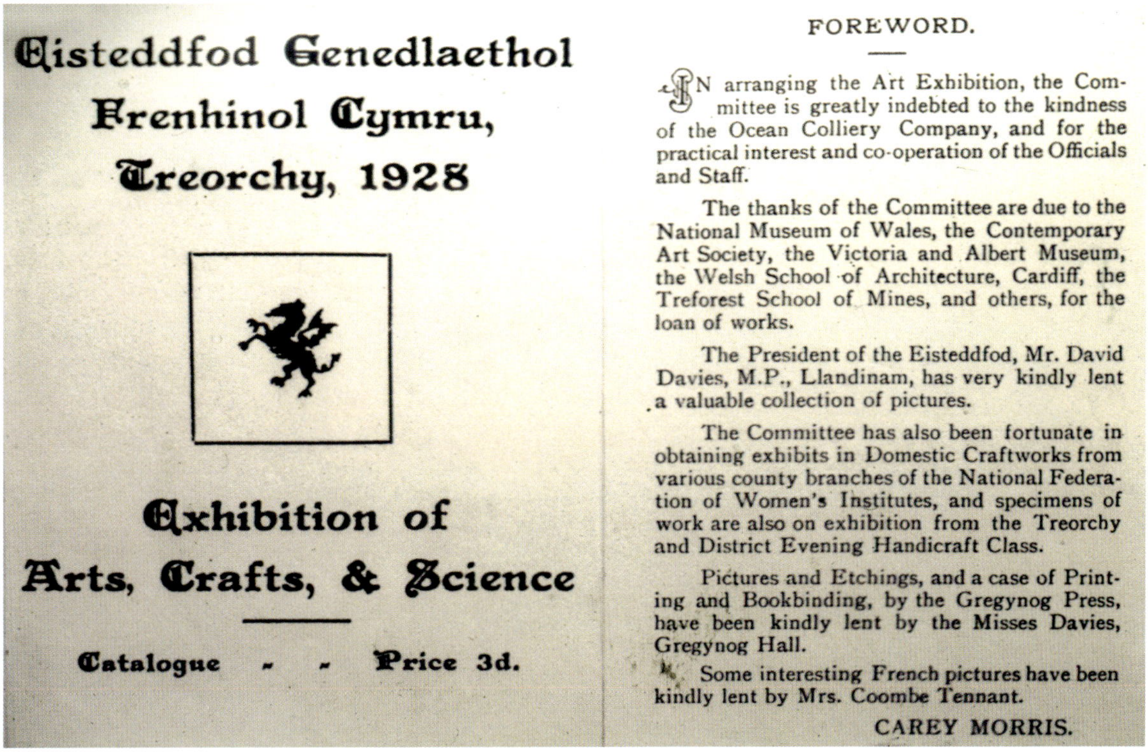

Eisteddfod Genedlaethol
Frenhinol Cymru,
Treorchy, 1928

Exhibition of
Arts, Crafts, & Science

Catalogue - - Price 3d.

FOREWORD.

IN arranging the Art Exhibition, the Committee is greatly indebted to the kindness of the Ocean Colliery Company, and for the practical interest and co-operation of the Officials and Staff.

The thanks of the Committee are due to the National Museum of Wales, the Contemporary Art Society, the Victoria and Albert Museum, the Welsh School of Architecture, Cardiff, the Treforest School of Mines, and others, for the loan of works.

The President of the Eisteddfod, Mr. David Davies, M.P., Llandinam, has very kindly lent a valuable collection of pictures.

The Committee has also been fortunate in obtaining exhibits in Domestic Craftworks from various county branches of the National Federation of Women's Institutes, and specimens of work are also on exhibition from the Treorchy and District Evening Handicraft Class.

Pictures and Etchings, and a case of Printing and Bookbinding, by the Gregynog Press, have been kindly lent by the Misses Davies, Gregynog Hall.

Some interesting French pictures have been kindly lent by Mrs. Coombe Tennant.

CAREY MORRIS.

Carey's foreword and programme cover to the Arts, Crafts, & Science exhibition of the National Eisteddfod of Wales in Treorci, 1928

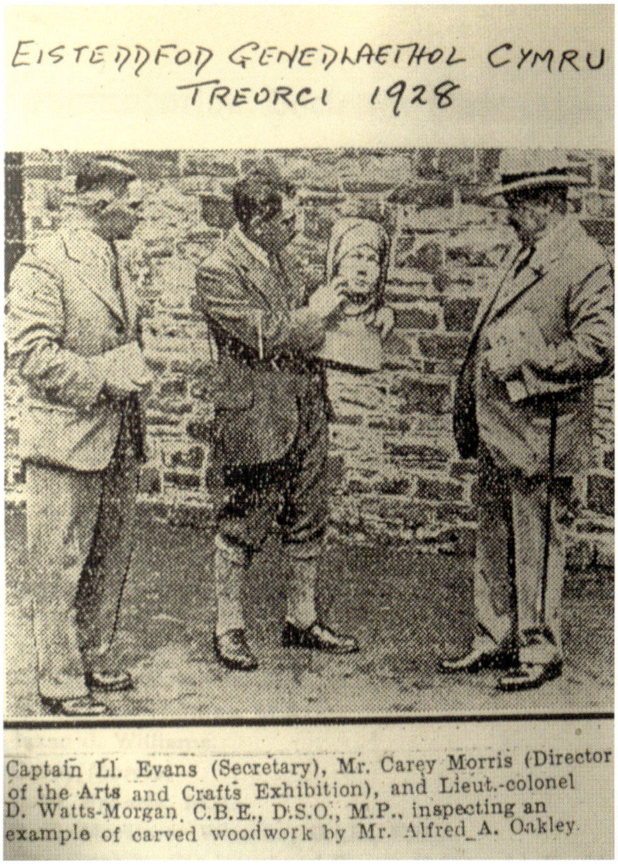

EISTEDDFOD GENEDLAETHOL CYMRU
TREORCI 1928

Captain Ll. Evans (Secretary), Mr. Carey Morris (Director of the Arts and Crafts Exhibition), and Lieut.-colonel D. Watts-Morgan, C.B.E., D.S.O., M.P., inspecting an example of carved woodwork by Mr. Alfred A. Oakley.

Carey with VIPs at Treorci Eisteddfod. Carey as director of the Arts & Crafts showing a wood carving to Capt. Ll. Evans, secretary and Lt Col. Watts-Morgan CBE DSO MP

5 INDIAN SUMMER

Interspersed with frequent visits to Llandeilo and Newlyn, Carey and his wife led a scintillating social life in London, moving in artistic and literary circles, both before and after World War I. At social gatherings Carey was much in demand as an accomplished cellist. They entertained artists such as Sir William Orpen, the fashionable portraitist; Stanhope Forbes, founder of the Newlyn School; Sir Frank Brangwyn, the muralist; Sir George Clausen, the landscape painter; as well as Ernest Proctor, Carey's old friend from Newlyn days, and his wife Dod Proctor, remembered as Newlyn's brilliant students. Other guests included Paul Nash, the war artist; Evan Walters, the young artistic genius; and Sir Hubert von Herkomer, painter of scenes of social concern. Incidentally, it was Herkomer who designed the Gorsedd robes, worn at important National Eisteddfod ceremonies to this day. Herkomer once said that there was no such thing as Welsh art, and Carey agreed saying: 'There never will be any Welsh art while we starve our own artists, who have to leave Wales to be trained and seldom return' summed up in the catchphrase 'No living art in Wales until artists can live in Wales'.

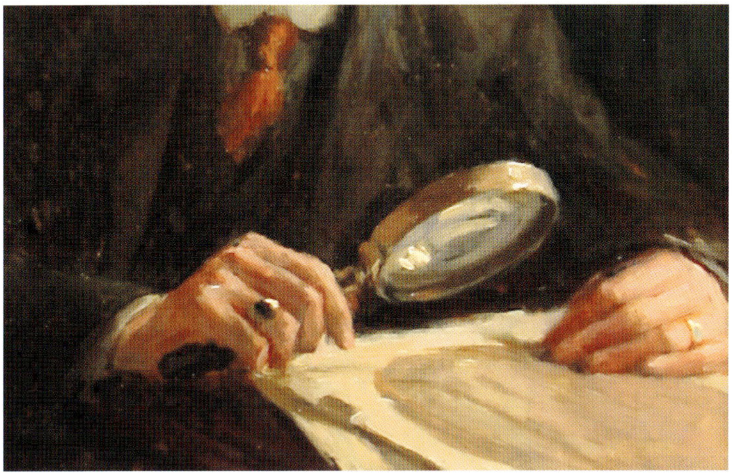

The Connoisseur – hands

In London, Carey had a studio in Cheyne Walk, Chelsea where he received many portrait commissions. Much like Augustus John, Carey was renowned for his portraits. The two artists had been friends for some years and it is said that Augustus told Carey that he wished he could draw hands as well as him and, occasionally, he asked Carey to draw the hands in portraits he himself was painting. Carey's skill in depicting hands is apparent in *The Connoisseur* and *Merfyn Williams*. When Carey moved back to Llandeilo on Jessie's death in 1936, Augustus John used to call at his house if he was in the neighbourhood.

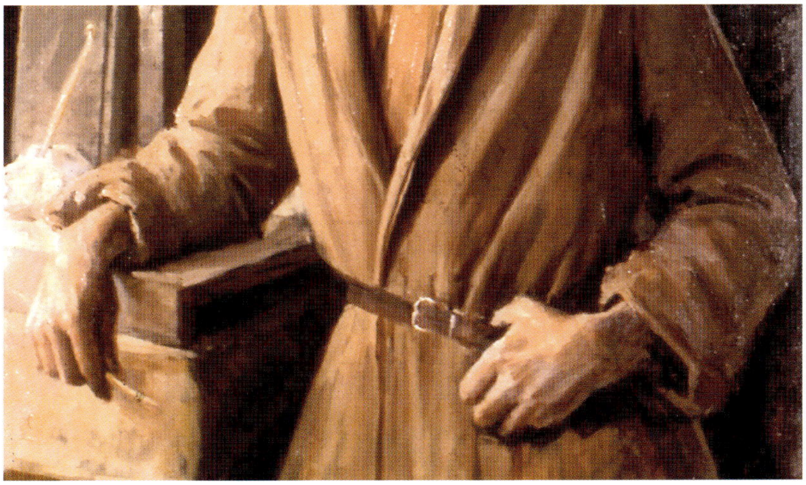

Merfyn Williams – hands

Although some portraitists tended to agree with Thomas Gainsborough who thought that 'Painting and punctuality mix like oil and vinegar', Carey sought to persuade his sitters to arrive on time, though he did not enforce this rule strictly. Carey needed his sitters to be in a *tranquil* mood and, when one of his well-heeled patrons always arrived late and stressed after driving through London traffic, Carey tactfully showed his disapproval. The man asked him what he could do, as he had so many commitments and was extremely busy. Carey advised him to employ a chauffeur. He did this, and from then on arrived on time in a relaxed frame of mind. An example of the tranquillity Carey desired in his sitters is the pastel portrait he composed of his sister Elizabeth, *Lizzie*.

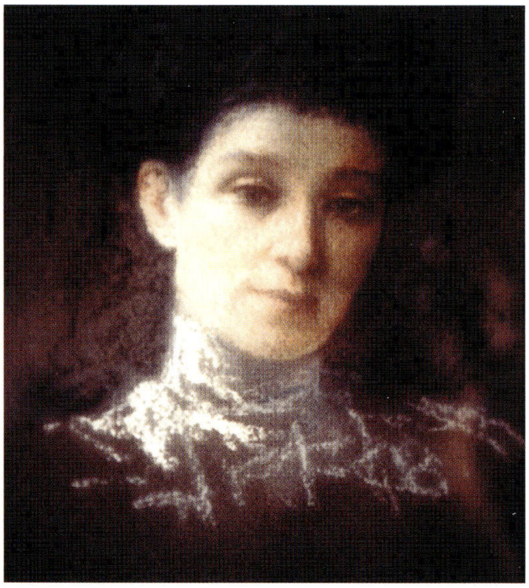

'Lizzie' Morris 12" x 10"

Carey Morris was a friend of the Lloyd-Johnes family who succeeded the Johnes family at Dolaucothi, Carmarthenshire, and was commissioned to paint a copy of the oil portrait of one their ancestors, *Thomas Johnes* (1721–80) of Llanfairclydogau, Ceredigion and Croft Castle, Herefordshire. This Thomas Johnes held the exalted office of *Custos Rotulorum* (Keeper of the Rolls) of Cardigan county, a position which meant he had the direct ear of the monarch on the affairs of the county. (Incidentally, he was also the father of the much-loved Squire Thomas Johnes (1748–1815) of Hafod, Ceredigion.) The original portrait had come into the possession of the Duke of Newcastle, and Carey's copy was displayed in the dining room of Dolaucothi, now sadly demolished, like so many country houses in Wales.

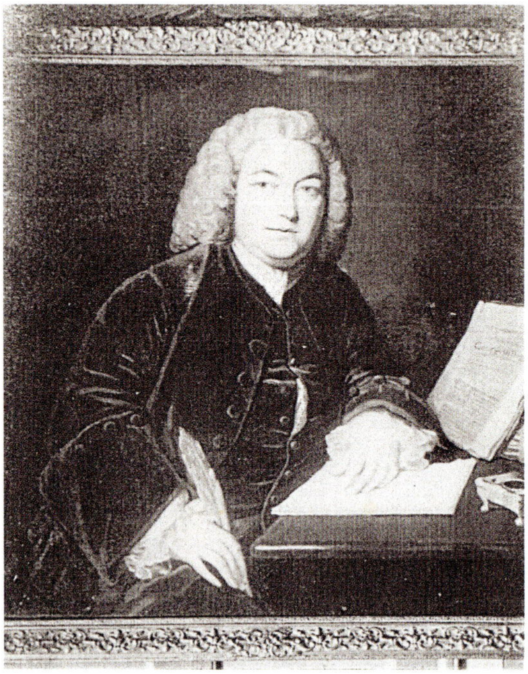

Thomas Johnes (1721–80)

Carey's copy was so true to the original that the family commissioned him in the 1930s to paint a posthumous portrait of *Judge John Johnes* (1800–76), the Squire of Dolaucothi, who was the great nephew of Thomas Johnes of Croft Castle. Judge John Johnes was brutally murdered by his butler. Carey created the portrait from a faded photograph, and succeeded in conveying in oils the compassionate and kind nature of the man who was beloved by his tenants for his fairness and consideration for their circumstances, and who was admired by everyone who knew

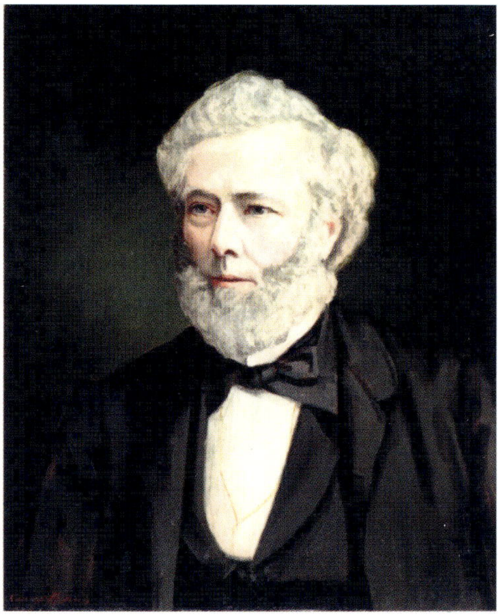

Judge John Johnes (1800–76) 1930s 26" x 22½"

him. The butler then tried to murder the judge's daughter and his own wife, before committing suicide. Both the judge and his murderer were buried in the same churchyard at Caio.

During the 1960s, my uncle, the Rev. Tawe Jones, poet, local historian and vicar of a neighbouring parish, took me to Caio churchyard and told me what had happened. So intense was the feeling of outrage that the murderer had been buried in the same churchyard as the much-loved judge that one dark night, some time later, the corpse of the murderer was disinterred and transported on a 'gambo' (a horse-drawn dray) a distance of over 20 miles and reburied in the pauper section of Llandulas churchyard. But when the people of Llandulas found out, they dug him up at the dead of night, loaded him on to a 'gambo', tied rags to the wheels to deaden the sound, and deposited the coffin back in Caio churchyard. Some say that he was reburied in Caio in an unmarked grave, but many believe the coffin was moved to a secret place. Whatever happened to the murderer's corpse, the whole unsavoury episode serves to demonstrate vividly the lengths to which the people of the neighbourhood were prepared to go in an attempt to alleviate, to some extent, the anger they felt at the brutal murder of their beloved squire and their revulsion that his murderer's body lay near to his, in the same consecrated ground. This story was confirmed to me many years later by my cousin, Canon David Jones, Chancellor of the Diocese of St Davids.

Carey was commissioned to portray *Sir Joseph Bradney*, one of the landed gentry of Gwent, who was knighted for his services to Wales in 1924. Sir Joseph was a classical scholar, a historian and author of the monumental reference work, *History of Monmouthshire*, compiled over many years, but

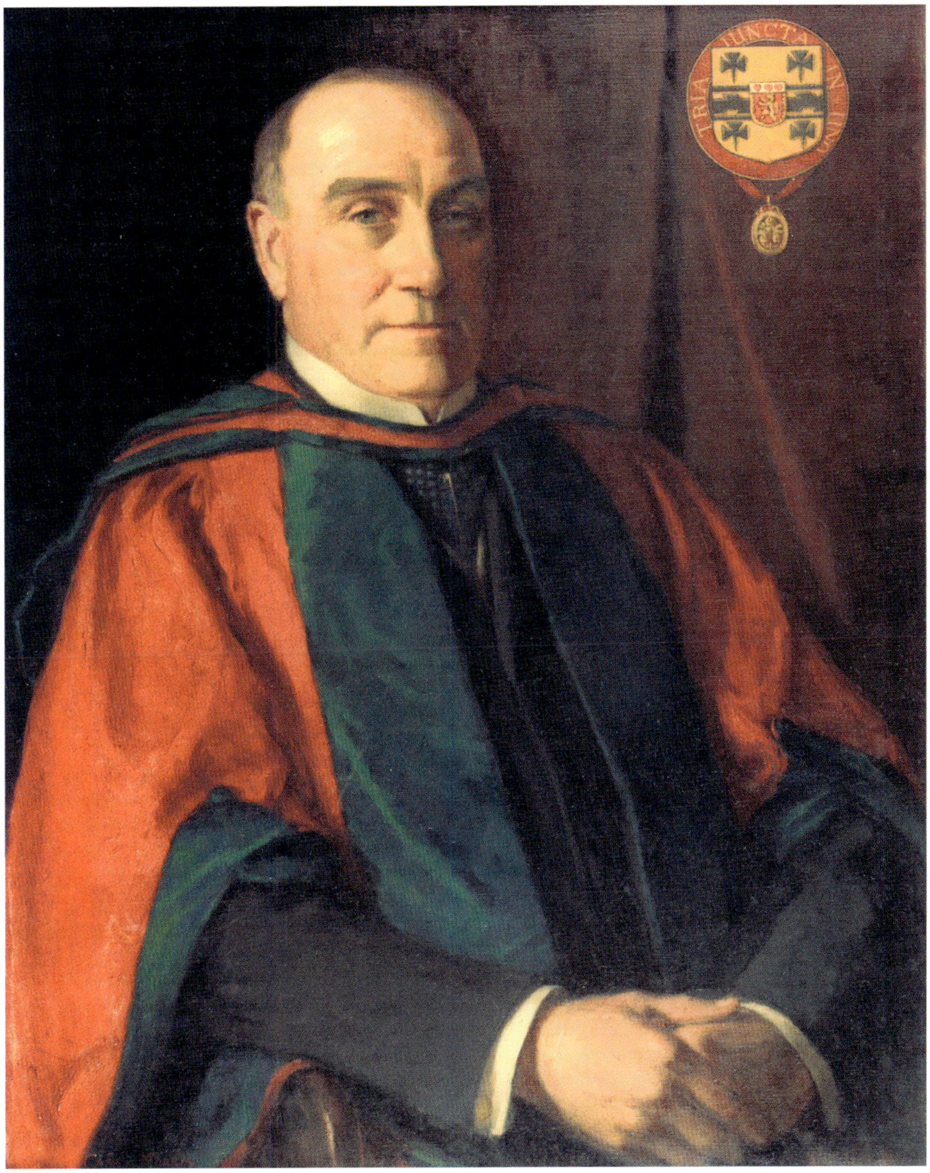

Sir Joseph Bradney 35½" x 27½"

incomplete at his death in 1933. Fortunately, the fifth and last volume was edited posthumously by Dr Madeleine Gray from his detailed notes. Sir Joseph wrote many books, including two in Latin. He learnt the Welsh language and his bardic title was 'Achydd Glan Troddi'. Like Carey he served in the army in Flanders during the World War I. While on active service in 1917 he wrote a collection of poetry and prose in Latin, *Noctes Flandricae*, and translated some parts into Welsh. He was an expert genealogist, and Carey, who was also interested in the subject, became a frequent visitor to Sir Joseph's home at Talycoed Court, Llanfihangel-Ystern-Llewern, Monmouth. Carey thought that it was through the intervention of Sir Joseph Bradney that the leek became the emblem, and 'Cymru am Byth' the motto, of the Welsh Guards.

Carey received many portrait commissions from well-known people at his Cheyne Walk studio. In 1920 he painted *Sir Vincent Evans*, C.H., who was a member of the team with Eleanor Roosevelt drafting the United Nations Charter for Human Rights before becoming a much respected judge at the European Court of Human Rights. Carey's painting portrays Sir Vincent's commanding presence, his leonine head and his authoritative bearing.

In 1924 he was commissioned to paint a portrait of *Rutland Boughton*, the composer of the great Celtic opera *The Immortal Hour*, which was described by Sir Edward Elgar as 'a work of genius'. George Bernard Shaw's opinion of Boughton's works was: 'Now that Elgar is gone, you have the only original personal English style on the market.' Boughton co-founded the Glastonbury Festival for Classical Music in 1914, and it ran successfully until 1926. He wrote five operas in the Arthurian cycle of music-dramas, as well as three symphonies and numerous other works. In his portrait, Carey reveals the thoughtful musician who created the new type of opera he called choral drama, but like Carey he has been largely neglected until now.

In 1928, Carey was commissioned by the residents of Llandeilo to design a flag representing the town to send to Llandilo, New South Wales, Australia. Llandeilo had previously received a fine silk flag as a gift from its 'daughter-town' of Llandilo. Unfortunately, that flag cannot now be found. Carey's extensive local knowledge and his deep sense of history made him the

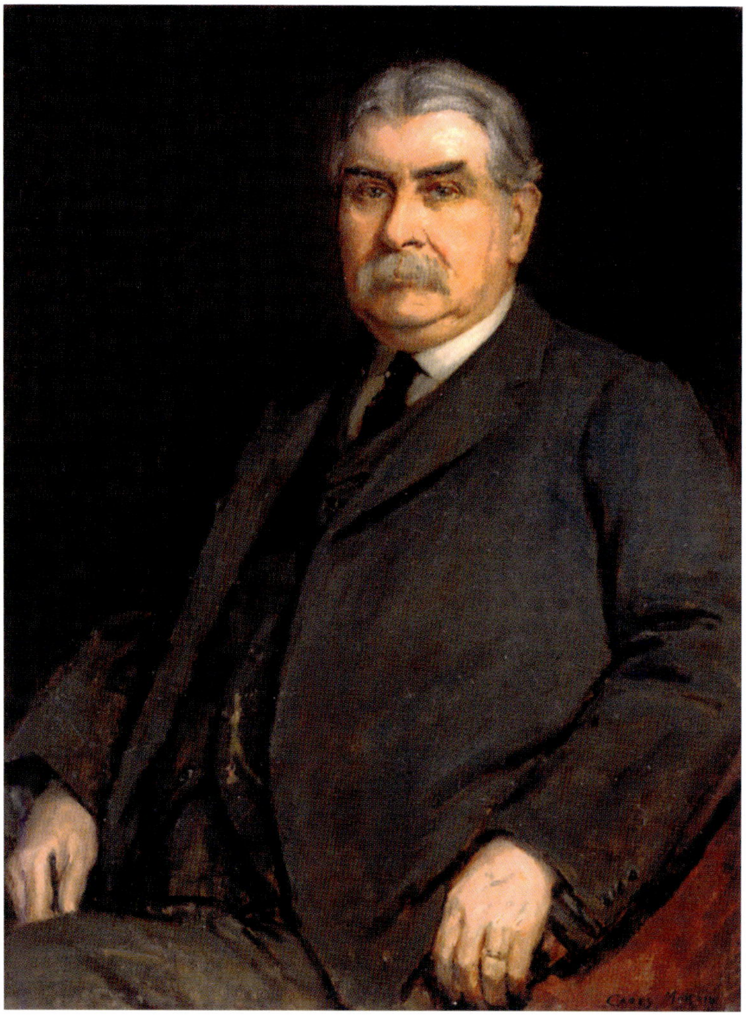

Sir Vincent Evans, C.H. 1924 39½" x 29½"

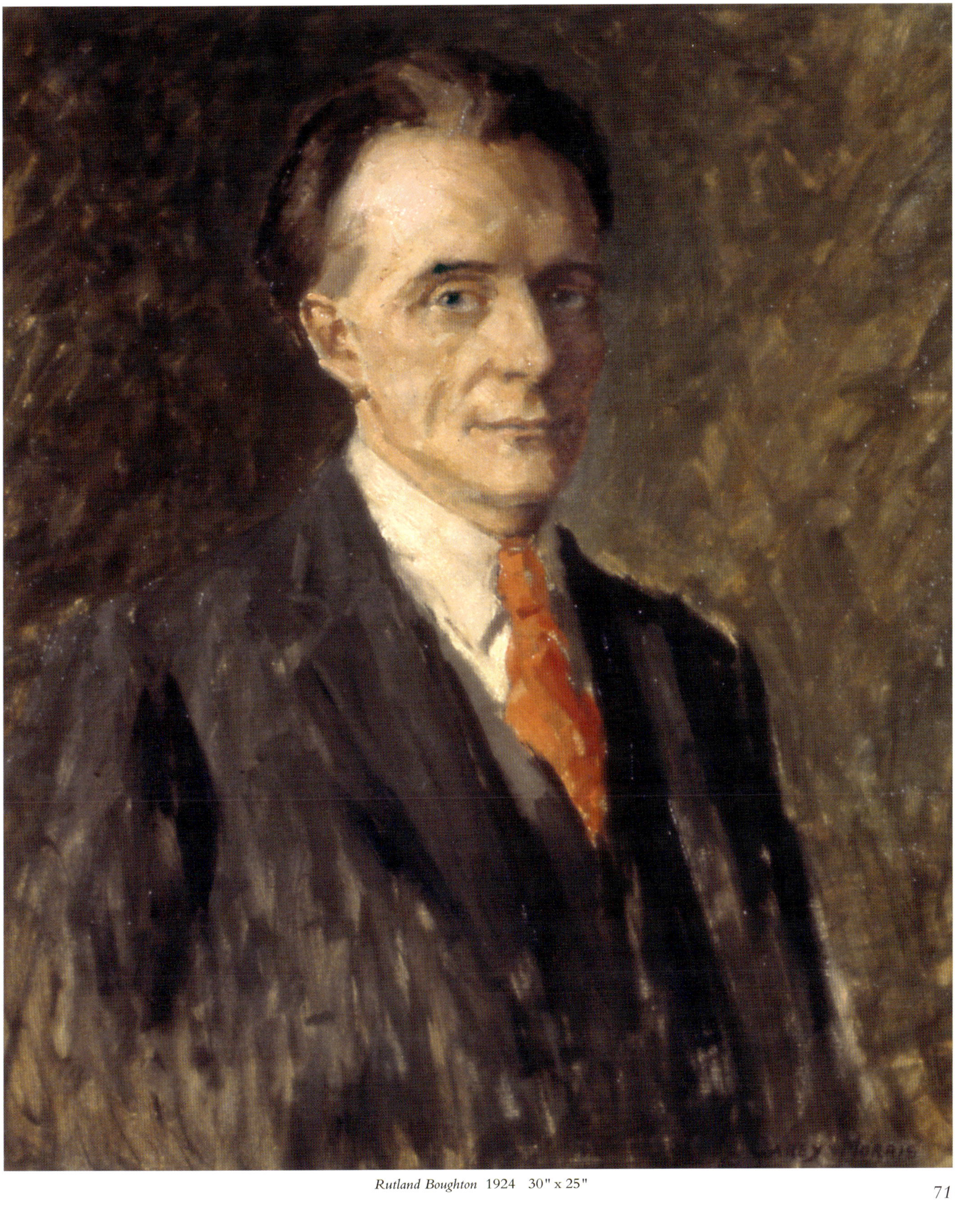

Rutland Boughton 1924 30" x 25"

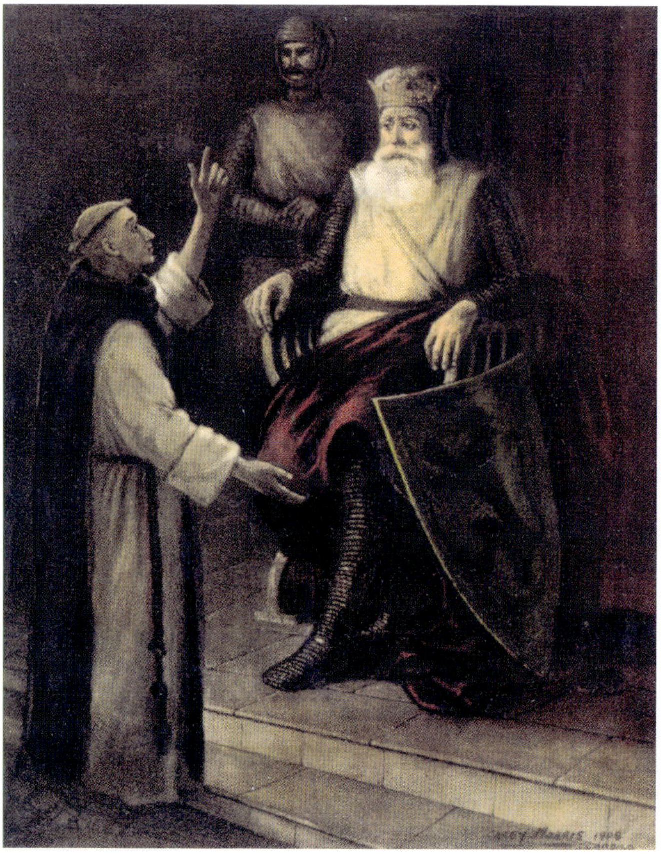

The Lord Rhys 1908

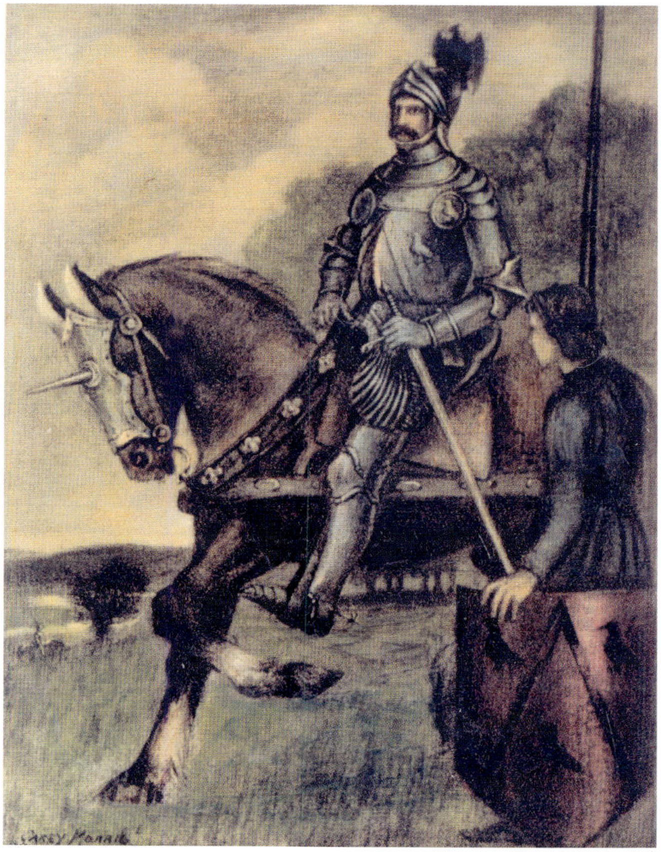

Sir Rhys ap Thomas 1908 14" x 11"

ideal person for the design assignment. In fact, 20 years previously, Carey had portrayed two of the greatest figures in Welsh history, both progenitors of the Lords Dynevor. The first was *The Lord Rhys* (d. 1197) and the second *Sir Rhys ap Thomas* (d. 1525). The Lord Rhys is shown crowned, enthroned and robed, receiving the supplication of a monk from one of the monasteries he founded, while one of his knights-at-arms stands behind the throne. Sir Rhys ap Thomas, Knight-banneret, is shown fully armed astride his charger and attended by his esquire who holds his shield.

The Llandeilo flag which Carey designed for Llandilo was made of silk and conforms to the usual custom, with the fly (length) twice as long as the dip (width). It measured nine feet by four and a half feet, large enough to accommodate all the elements Carey painted on the royal blue obverse side. He included Henry VII's royal coat of arms, a picture of Sir Rhys ap

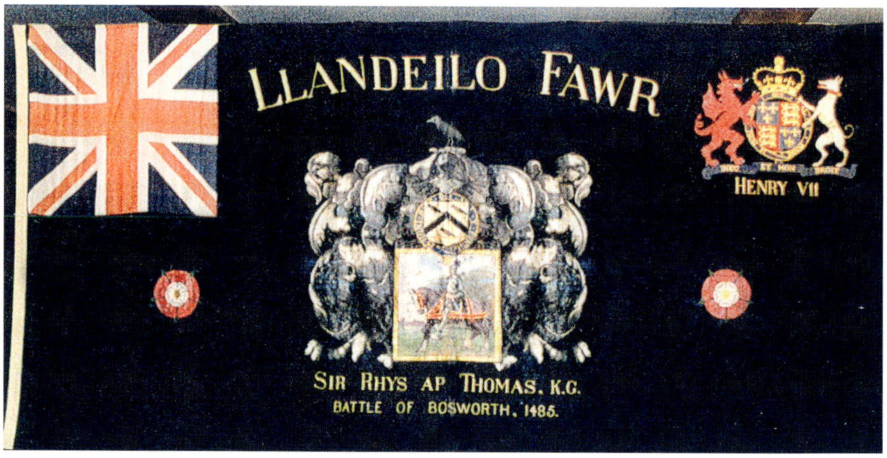

The Llandeilo flag 1928 54" x 108"

Thomas with his coat of arms, two Tudor roses together with appropriate captions, but also in the top left-hand corner, as a gesture, a Union flag of flawed dimensions.

The silk standard of Henry Tudor, who became Henry VII, bore the red dragon of Cadwaladr, King of Britain in the seventh century. Henry VII claimed descent from Cadwaladr (d. 664) via Rhodri Mawr (d. 878) and The Lord Rhys of Dinefwr (d. 1197). Carey took delight in the fact that Rhys ap Thomas of Llandeilo, who had inherited the Dinefwr estates, was largely responsible for securing the throne for Henry Tudor, grandson of Sir Owain Tudor of Penmynydd, Anglesey. The House of Tudor is the greatest royal dynasty ever to reign in Britain, with the arts, education and commerce flourishing as never before. Like many historians Carey believed the Battle of Bosworth in 1485 was as much a Welsh conquest of England as the Battle of Hastings in 1066 had been a Norman conquest of England – Hastings placed a Norman dynasty on the throne and Bosworth placed a Welsh dynasty on the throne. With this in mind, Carey painted the coat of arms of King Henry VII in the top right-hand corner of his flag. The king's shield was supported by the red dragon of Wales and the silver greyhound of Henry's mother. Incidentally, all the Tudor monarchs used the red dragon of Wales as a supporter, but when the Stuarts came to the throne in 1603, they replaced the ancient Welsh dragon of Cadwaladr with their unicorn, but the dragon still reigns in venerable establishments, such as King's College Chapel, Cambridge and Eton College.

During the Wars of the Roses, Wales supported the red rose of Lancaster against the white rose of York, and the victory of the Welshman Henry Tudor, under his red dragon standard at the Battle of Bosworth, rid the realm of the hated Yorkist Richard III. Six months after his coronation, King Henry VII married Elizabeth of York and combined the red and white roses to form the Tudor Rose, which he adopted as one of his emblems. This signified that he had brought to an end the Wars of the Roses which had decimated the land for over 30 years – hence the Tudor Roses on either side of the central raven on the coat of arms on the Llandeilo flag. Though Englishmen regard King Henry VII's marriage as a union of the two roses, Welshmen, natural genealogists, regard it as the union of a descendant of The Lord Rhys of Dinefwr with the heiress of Llywelyn the Great. At the end of his reign Henry VII left behind him a land peaceful and orderly, the nobility tamed and the treasury fuller than ever before. He had saved the country from sinking into anarchy.

The centre of the flag displays the coat of arms of Sir Rhys ap Thomas K.G. of Dinefwr who was a descendant of The Lord Rhys. Their shield and crest are now borne by Lord Dynevor. On the shield is a chevron between three black ravens and the crest is a black raven. Urien Rheged, who lived in the sixth century, was reputed to be a progenitor of the House of Dinefwr and it is said that his son, Owain ab Urien, was accompanied to the wars by an 'unkindness of ravens' which were bred in Dinefwr, surely better than a 'murder of crows'!

Five centuries later when the Tower of London was being built, tradition has it that an 'unkindness of ravens' arrived from Dinefwr to guard the Tower. Whenever a raven died in the Tower a replacement arrived from the Round Tower at Dinefwr – hence the ravens on the Dinefwr coat of arms. The Raven Master at the Tower of London told me of the six ravens presently at the Tower of London, four still have Welsh names – Rhys, Gwilym, Cedric and Branwen. In 1660 King Charles II ordered the ravens in the Tower to be destroyed but he was apprised of the legend that if the ravens ever left the Tower there would be dire consequences – the Tower would fall and the monarchy would crumble. Remembering that his father had been beheaded in 1649, he decreed that six ravens with clipped wings be kept in the Tower in perpetuity. In the 1930s a Nazi official ridiculed the Tower ravens when comparing them with Germany's eagles, and was then duly bitten by one of the ravens. In the spring of 2001 an eminent veterinary surgeon recalled how he had received what amounted to a monarchical command to minister to a Tower raven which had lost its right leg. After fitting a wooden leg it was able to walk and soon learnt to use its artificial leg as a strut when it perched.

On the Llandeilo flag encircling the shield of Sir Rhys ap Thomas is the 'Garter', denoting a Knight of the Garter, the highest order of knighthood in Britain. The Garter emblem and motto are said to owe their origin to an occasion when King Edward III either replaced a lady's garter around her leg, or put it around his own leg, saying to the amused onlookers, as he could hardly speak English, *Honi soit qui mal y pense* – 'evil be to him who evil thinks'! Surmouting the shield is the knight-banneret's helmet, crowned with a wreath upon which stands the black raven crest. Issuing from beneath the wreath, and investing the picture of Sir Rhys ap Thomas K.G., is an elaborated representation of the mantling, or tattered silken draping, worn to protect the nape of the neck from the sun. Carey painted Sir Rhys ap Thomas in a complete suit of armour, the raven crest perched on the wreath above his helmet, his charger caparisoned in scarlet. Underneath is the inscription 'Sir Rhys ap Thomas, K.G. Battle of Bosworth, 1485' and above, 'Llandeilo Fawr', all in gilt letters. To Sir Rhys ap Thomas belongs the credit for having slain, in the Battle of Bosworth in 1485, the treacherous tyrant Richard III.

The reverse of the flag is the national flag of Wales – a red dragon on a silver and green background. There is, however, a small courtesy square Union flag in the top left-hand corner. It might be considered somewhat incongruous that the flag devised by Carey in 1928 depicting the dragon of Cadwaladr which was over 1,300 years old and the ravens of Urien Rheged which were over

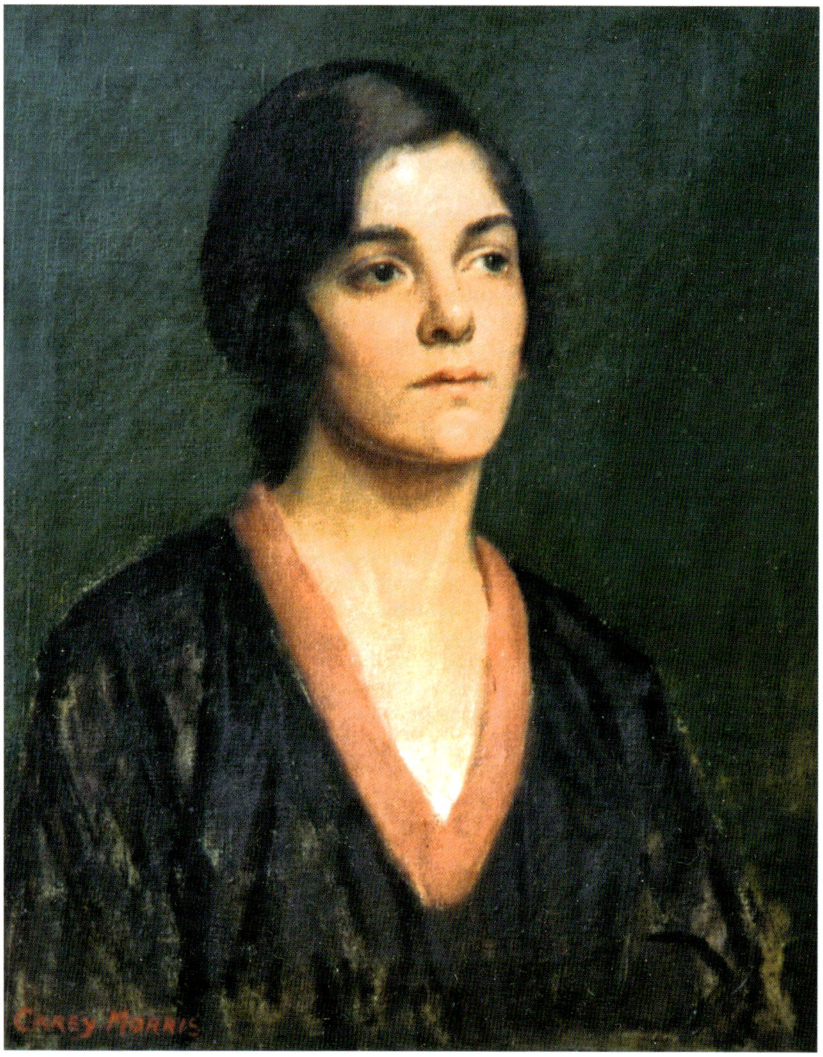

The Hon. Imogen Rhys, daughter of Lord Dynevor 20" x 16"

1,400 years old, should also show the Union flag which had been cobbled together only 127 years previously – even the Tudor Rose was almost 450 years old – but then Carey was ever charitable. (Interestingly, the Union flag is commonly called the Union 'Jack' because it was hoisted by the sailor jacks when they arrived in port to drink the taverns dry.)

In 1928, Carey's flag was unfurled in Llandeilo by the 7th Lord Dynevor, who was 16th in descent from Sir Rhys ap Thomas, and on the distaff side was a descendant of The Lord Rhys himself. Lord Dynevor was the son-in-law of a former Governor of New South Wales. Carey's portrait of the *Hon. Imogen Rhys*, daughter of Lord Dynevor shows a sensitive, pensive young lady. In his address Lord Dynevor said he was very proud that the arms of the House of Dynevor were displayed on the flag. Both the Llandeilo flag and the Llandilo flag were dedicated by the vicar of Llandeilo, archdeacon of Carmarthen. The ceremony of flags was followed by a march-past of civic dignitaries, Red Cross nurses, schoolchildren and Girl Guides. Carey's flag was then sent from Tilbury Docks, London on the *S.S. Chitral* (Orient Line) to Llandilo Public School in Australia, which was founded in 1866.

In the 1860s many parents in New South Wales did not appreciate the inestimable value of education and the Board of National Education summed up the attitude of the majority of parents thus: 'We are not particularly desirous to obtain education for our children in as much as they are useful to us at home – but we shall have no objection to sending them to school when they can be spared.' However the people of Llandilo did not subscribe to this view and petitioned for the establishment of a school in 1865 and Llandilo Public School opened in 1866.

Similarly, the people of Llandeilo were civic-minded enough to want their children to be educated. They were fortunate that the 4th Lord Dynevor became their munificent benefactor. He, at his sole expense, gave Llandeilo its first primary school in 1865. So the two schools are practically the same age, although Llandeilo, having existed for about 1,300 years, can claim to be the 'mother-town' of Llandilo, which is not yet 160 years old.

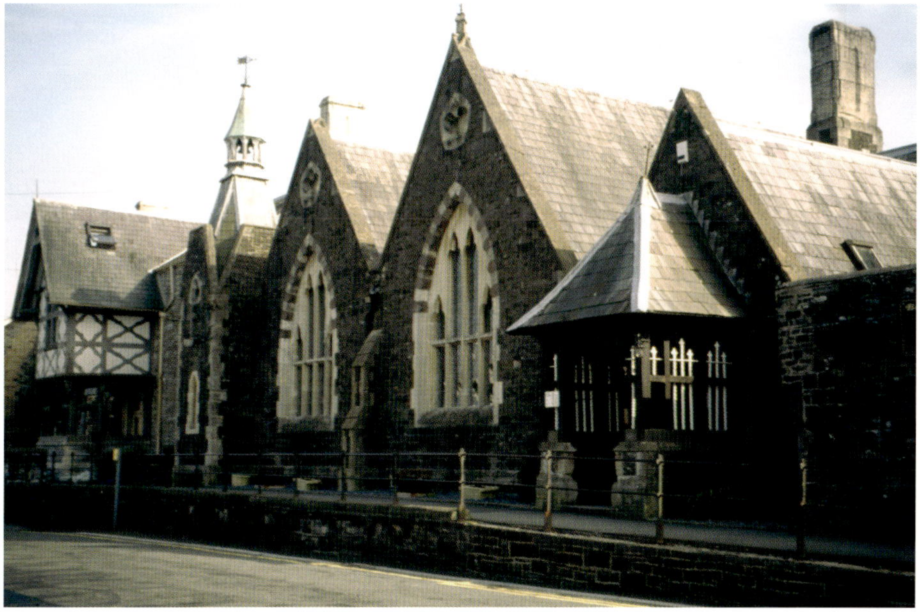

Llandeilo Primary School

Carey Morris' flag, which conveys so much history in the symbolism of its artistry, was dedicated and unfurled in Llandilo on 4 June 1928 in the presence of about 400 people, many of them of Welsh descent, and some from Llandeilo. From Sydney came members of the Honourable Society of Cymmrodorion together with the Welsh Choral Society, and the ceremony opened with the singing of the Welsh National

Anthem. After the dedication of the flag, the choir gave a stirring rendition of the 'Men of Harlech'. The ceremony of unfurling the flag was performed by the Hon. Albert Bruntnell, Chief Secretary of the Government and a native of Wales. There followed a convivial reception and, after a splendid luncheon with many toasts, the choir led the community singing.

A few years ago my daughter visited Llandilo and saw Carey's flag prominently displayed in the school library at Llandilo Public School. Although the bond forged between Llandeilo and Llandilo over three-quarters of a century ago became rather tenuous at one time, Carey would have been delighted that the links are now becoming stronger. In the last 25 years

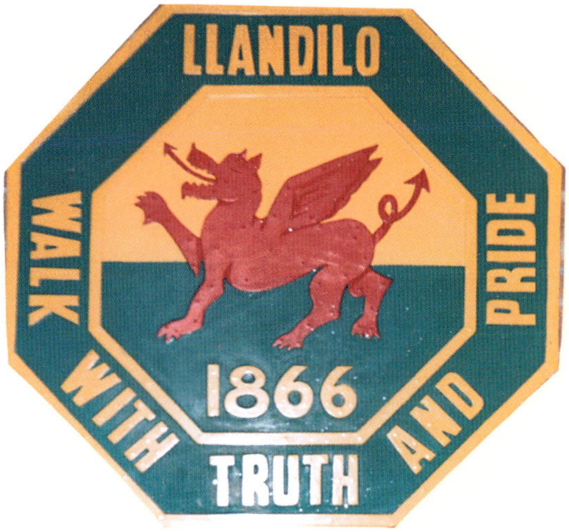

Llandilo Public School badge

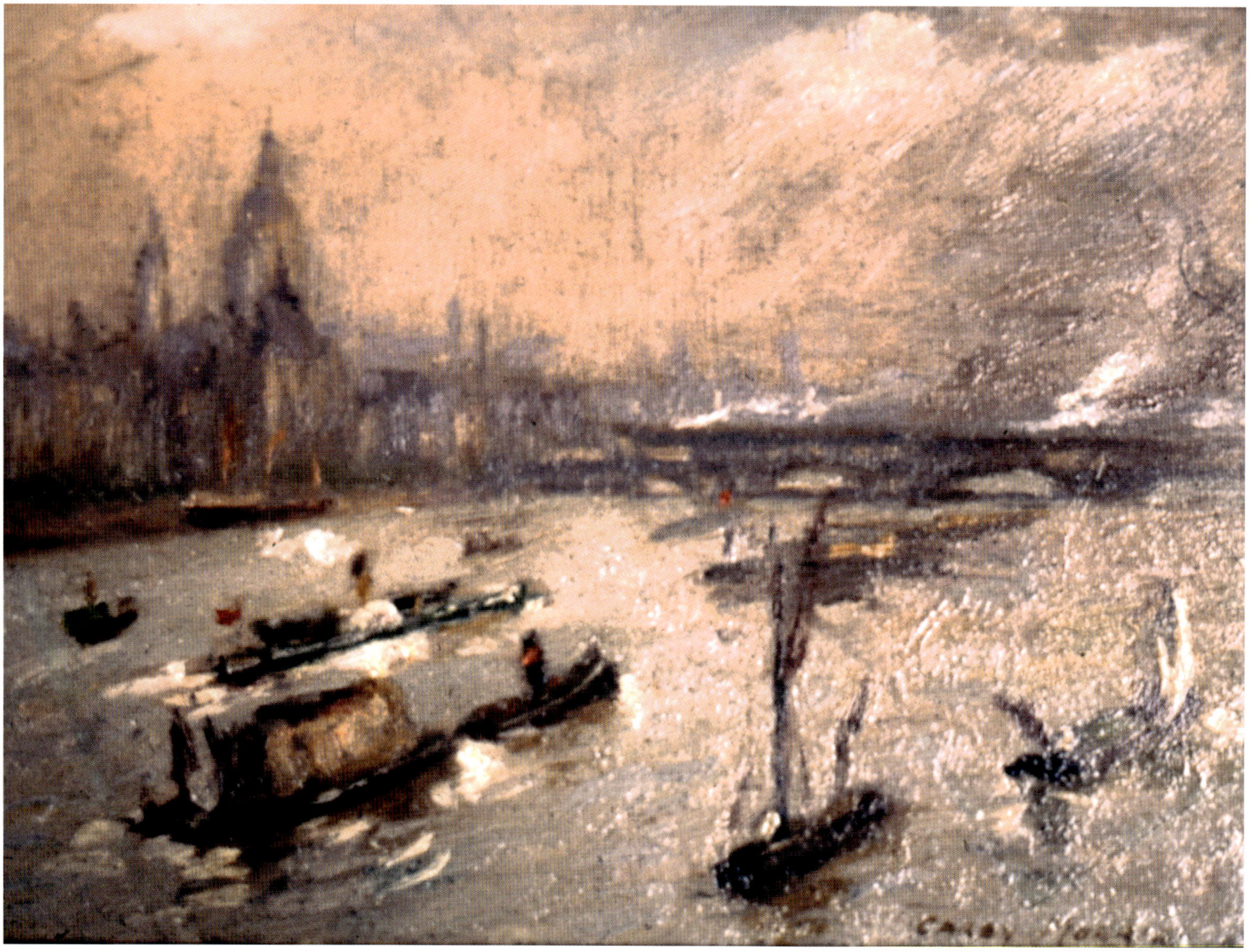

River Thames and St Paul's 1930s 6" x 8½"

exchange visits have occurred and, during the Rugby World Cup in Cardiff in 1999, visitors from Llandilo wearing the victorious Australian rugby shirts, were welcomed at Llandeilo Primary School. The pupils of the two schools now correspond as pen pals. The Llandilo Public School badge as well as the badges worn by captains, prefects and house captains is a Welsh dragon. The names of their four school houses are Bangor, Caernarvon, Denbigh and Glamorgan. Let us hope that the links between the two schools will become ever stronger, and that the Llandilo school motto, 'Walk with Truth and Pride', will always guide the pupils of both schools.

★ ★ ★ ★

While living in London Carey produced a few paintings of urban scenes: two are in impressionistic style: *River Thames and St Paul's* and *River Thames with the Houses of Parliament.* Another two depict scenes in the Inner Temple: *Fountain Court* and *Pump Court.* There is also Carey's *Garden in Highgate.*

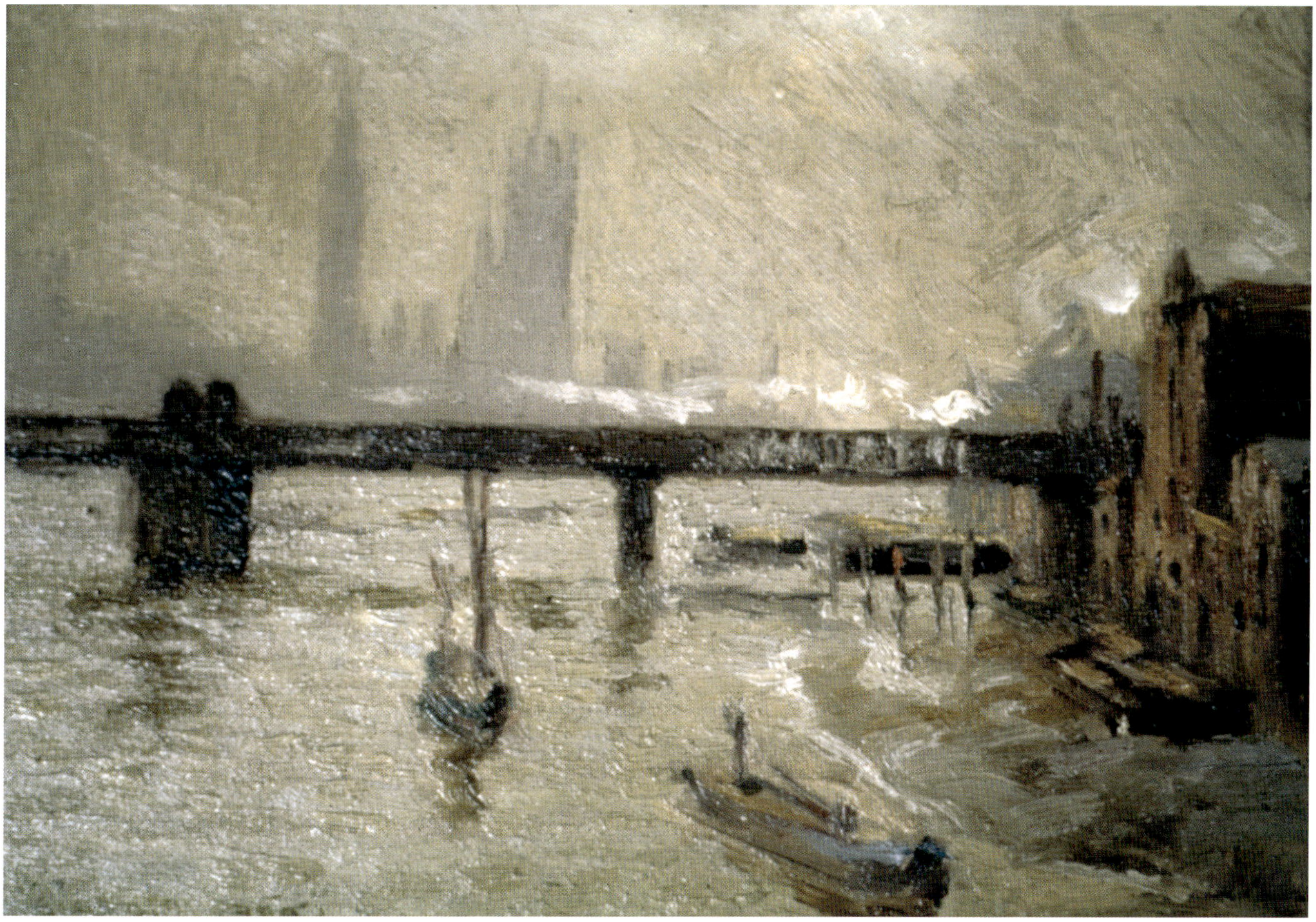

River Thames with the Houses of Parliament 1930s 6" x 8½"

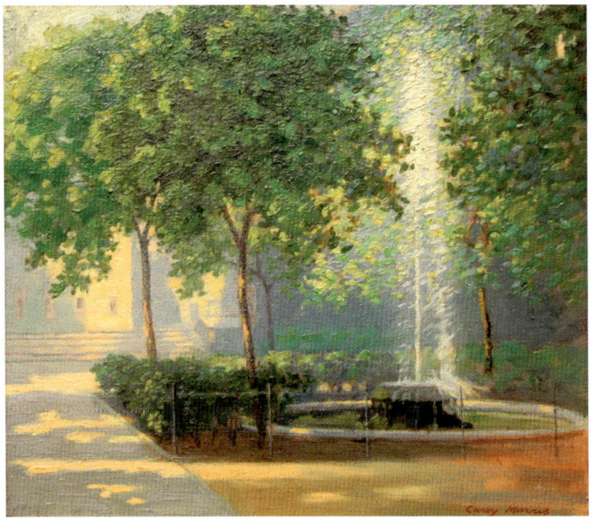

Fountain Court, Inner Temple
1920 15¼" x 17½"

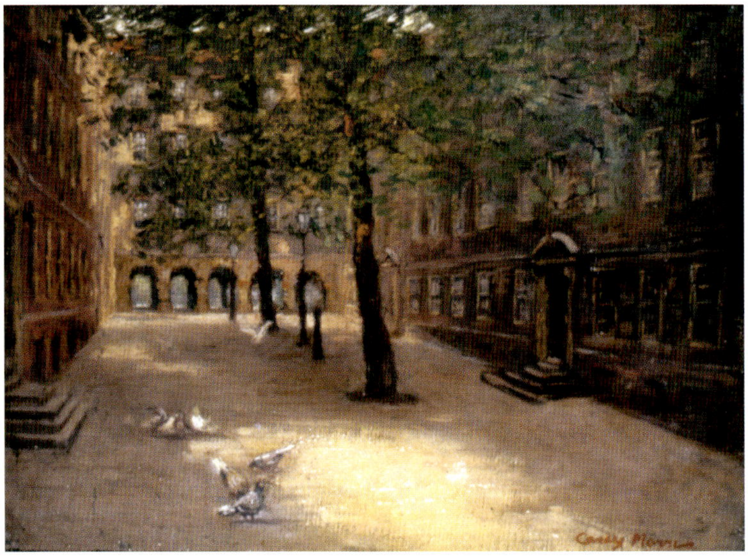

Pump Court, Inner Temple
1920 15½" x 19½"

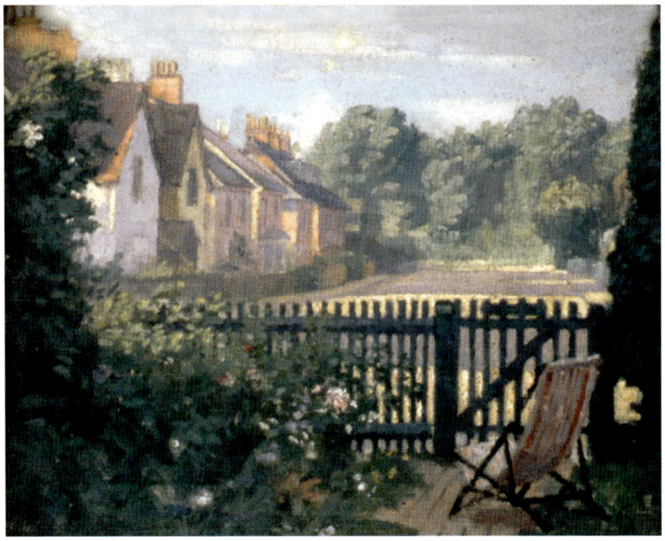

Garden in Highgate
1930 12" x 14"

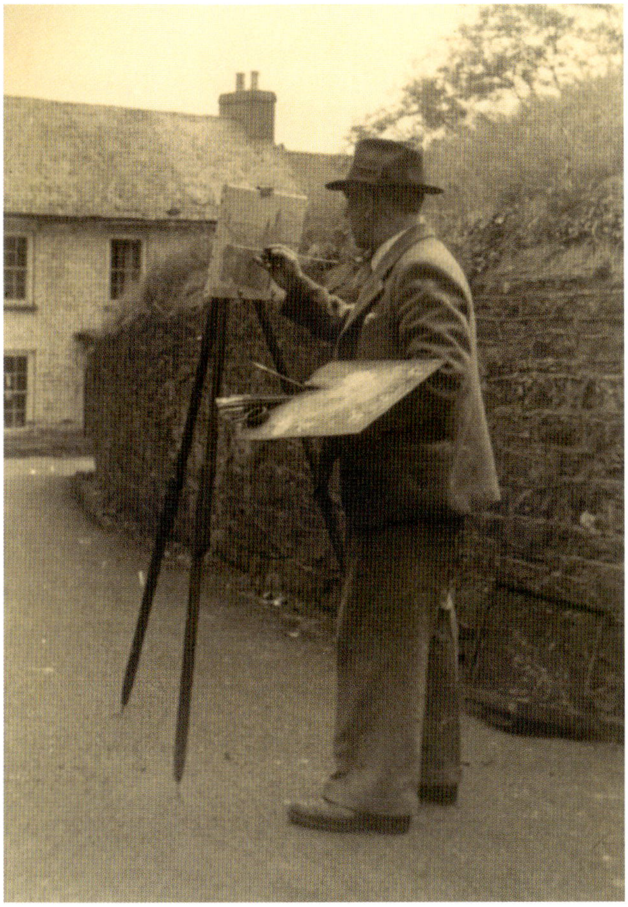

Carey painting Church Street, Llandeilo

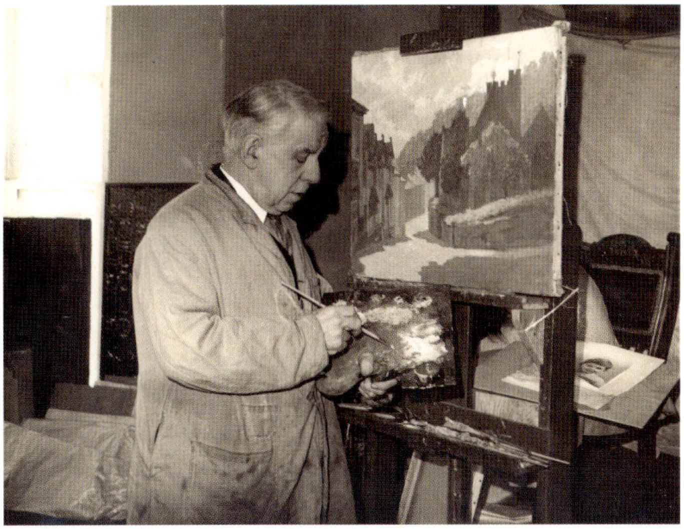

Carey completing *Church Street* in studio

On his return to Llandeilo he painted some memorable pictures of his home town. There are photographs of Carey painting *Church Street*. He also painted *Llandeilo Bridge* and *A Path in Dynevor Park*. There is a panoramic view from the castle, *Ox-bowing of the River Tywi* as seen through the eyes of the man standing at the reconstructed south curtain wall overlooking a precipitous drop. Nor far away is the magnificently situated Carreg Cennen Castle built by The Lord Rhys, reputedly on the site of the fort established by Urien Rheged. Carey made a striking silhouette, *Carreg Cennen Castle*.

In Llandeilo in the 1920s Carey often used Llanwenog-born David Evans, a likeable character in his eighties, as a model. He was a skilled millwright who was able to solve some not unduly complicated problems with the machinery of that time. My grandfather, who occasionally employed him on his farms, considered him to be a most intelligent man. David Evans was generally known as 'Dafi'r Felin' [Dafi of the mill] and was an impressive looking man and a familiar figure throughout south-west Wales. Carey told me of an incident when Lord Dynevor was bidding farewell to his guest, Field Marshal Lord Roberts of Kandahar, V.C. at Llandeilo railway station in the 1900s, Lord Roberts enquired, 'Who's that fine looking fellow over there?'

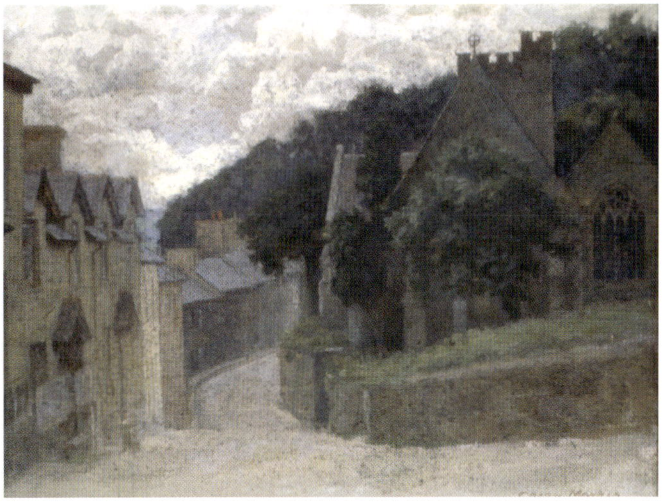

Church Street, Llandeilo after 1936 13" x 17"

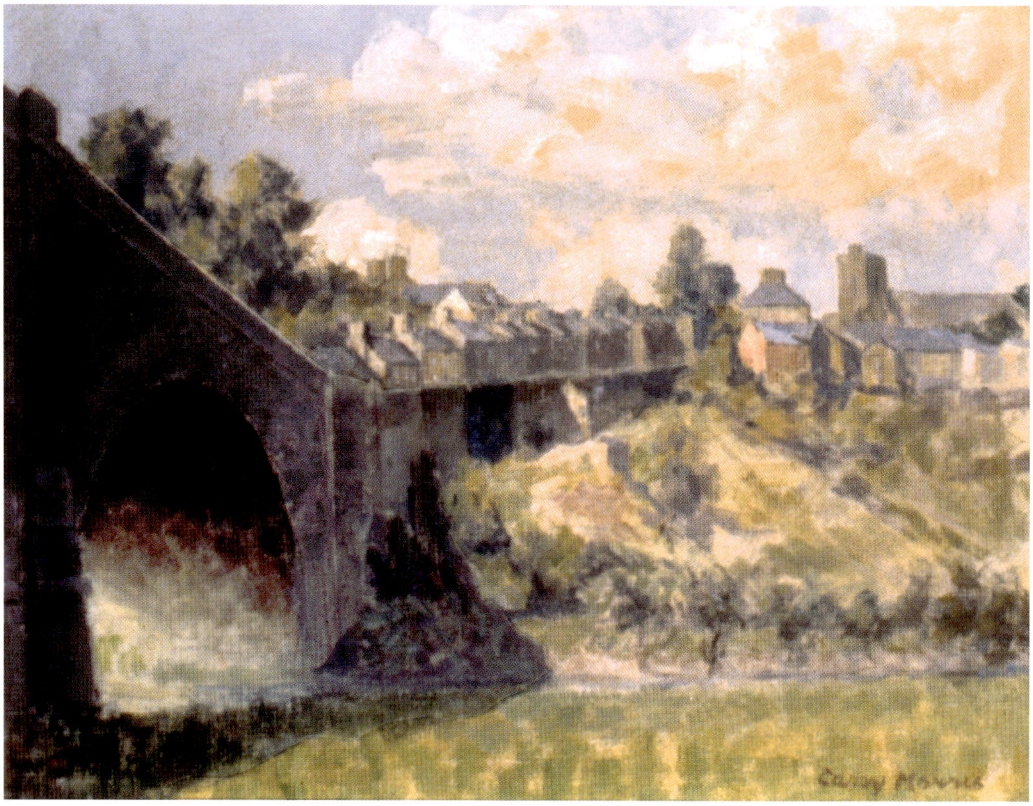

Llandeilo Bridge after 1936 15½" x 19½"

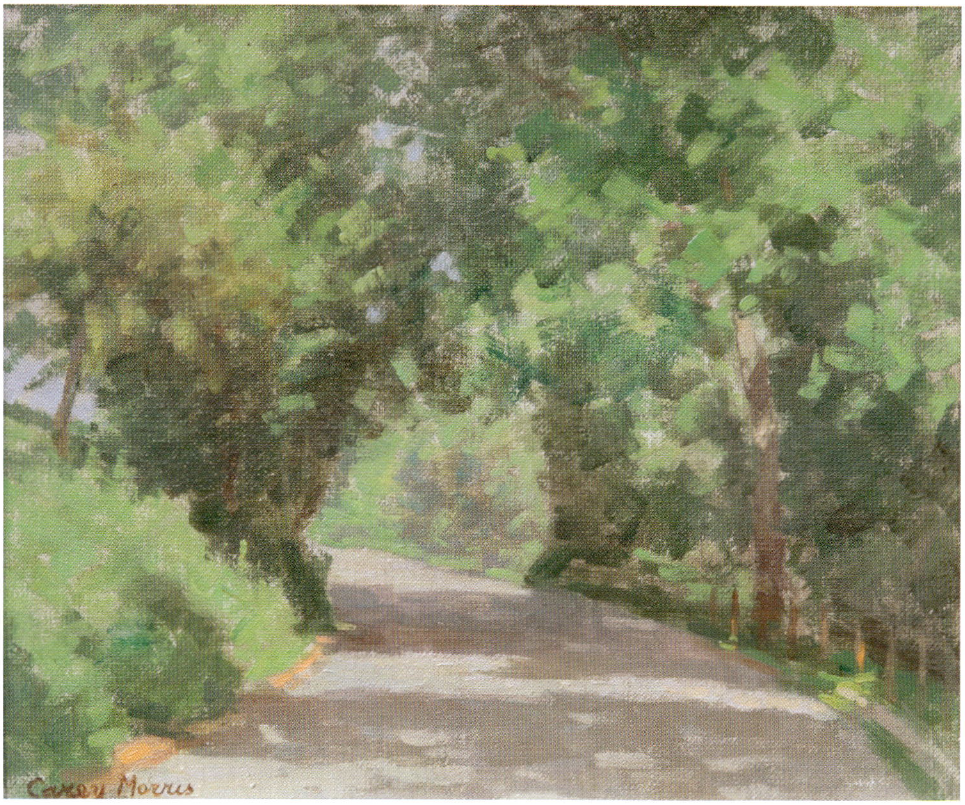

A Path in Dynevor Park after 1936 11½" x 13"

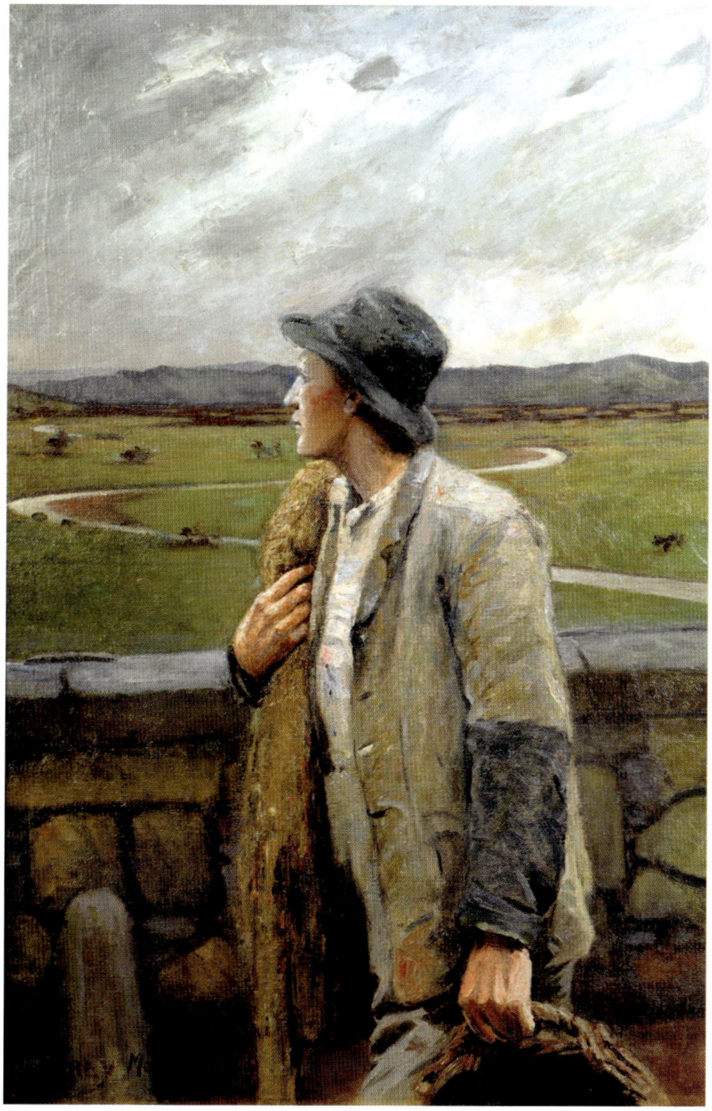

Ox-bowing of the River Tywi 1912 35" x 22"

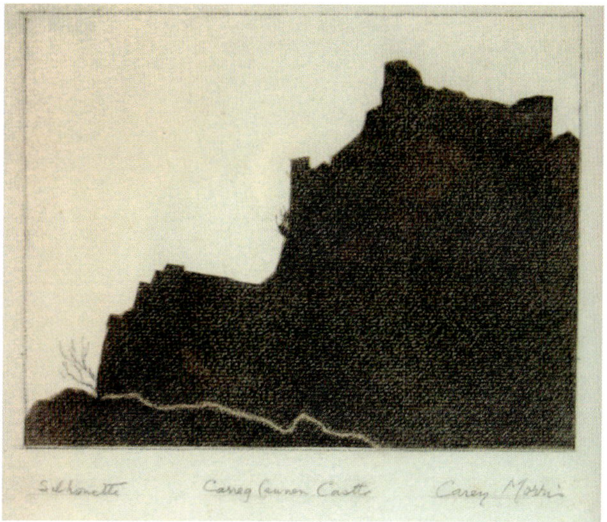

Carreg Cennen Castle 10½" x 10"

'Fine looking fellow be damned', said Lord Dynevor, 'He's the wiliest poacher for miles around!' In fact, Carey painted Dafi'r Felin in many guises: *House Decorator*, *Cellist* and *Fisherman*.

Commenting on Carey's work, Sir Kyffin Williams wrote: 'The main beneficial influence on his work comes from Stanhope Forbes who was, I believe, the most important figure in the Newlyn School. Forbes too has been neglected, for he was a strong and fluid handler of paint.' Referring to Carey's painting of Dafi'r Felin when acting the part of a house decorator, Sir Kyffin continued: 'This spontaneous fluidity can be seen in the smaller work of Carey Morris, as in his "Dafi of the Mill". Spontaneity is, I believe, a characteristic in Welsh painting.'

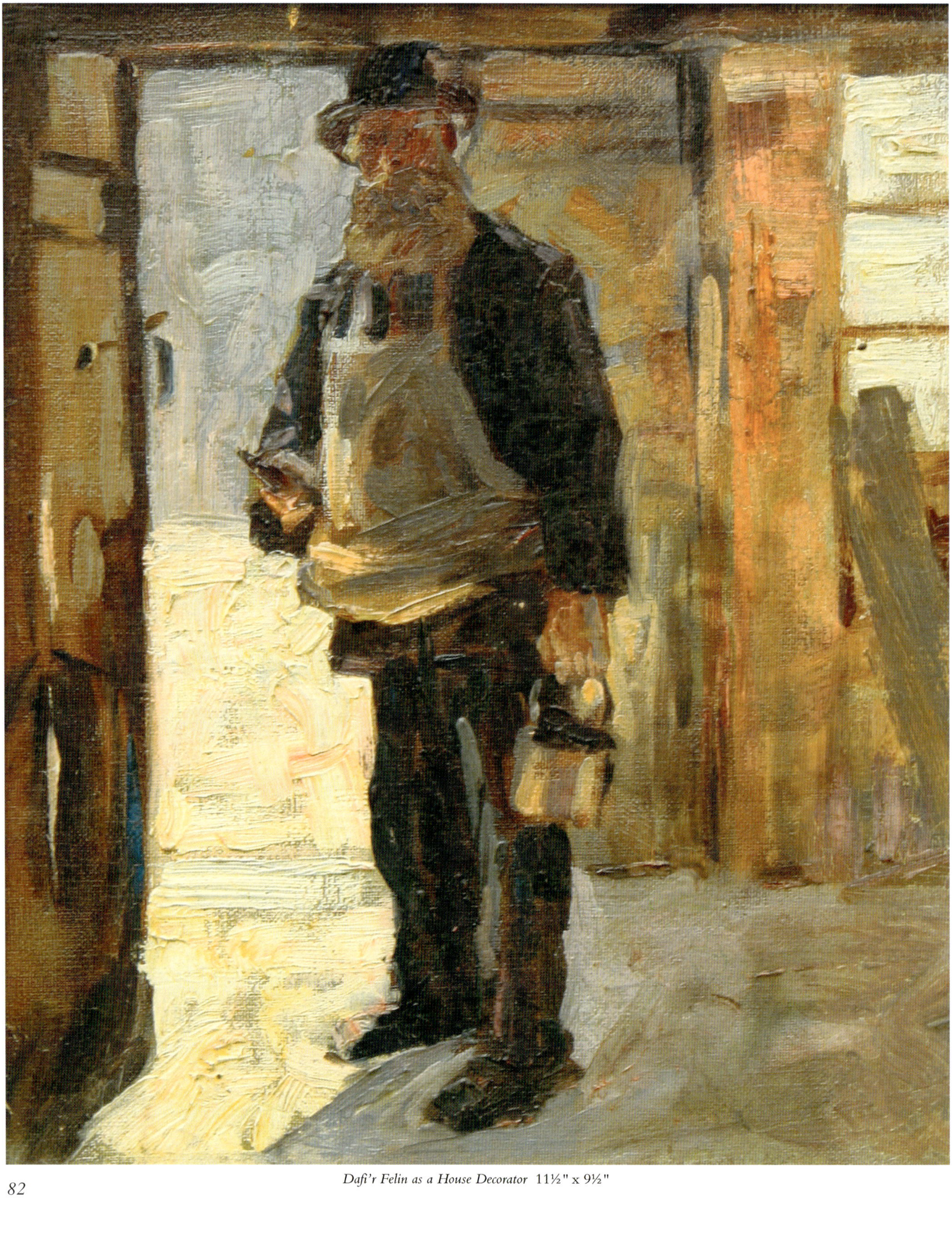

Dafi'r Felin as a House Decorator 11½" x 9½"

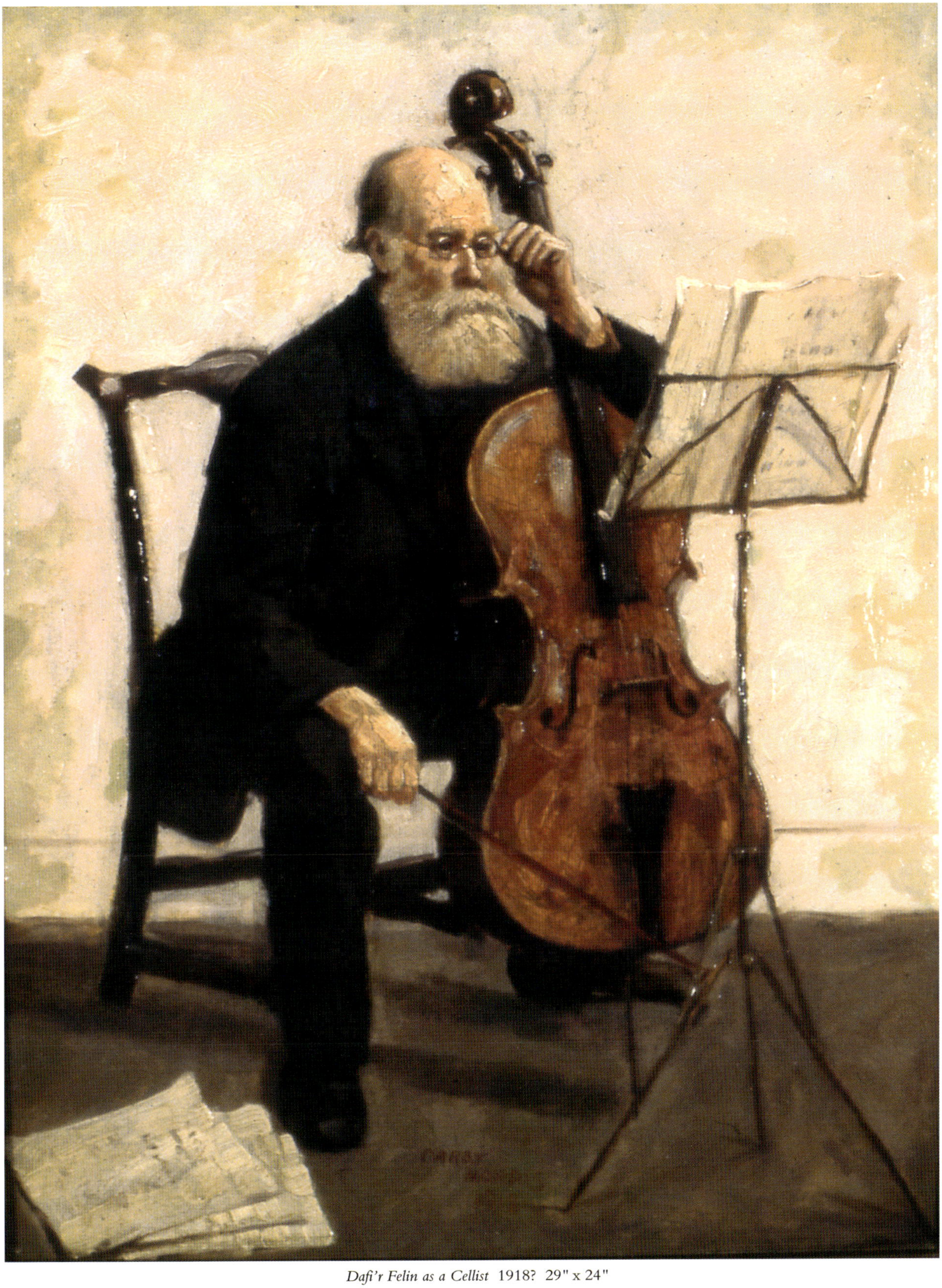

Dafi'r Felin as a Cellist 1918? 29" x 24"

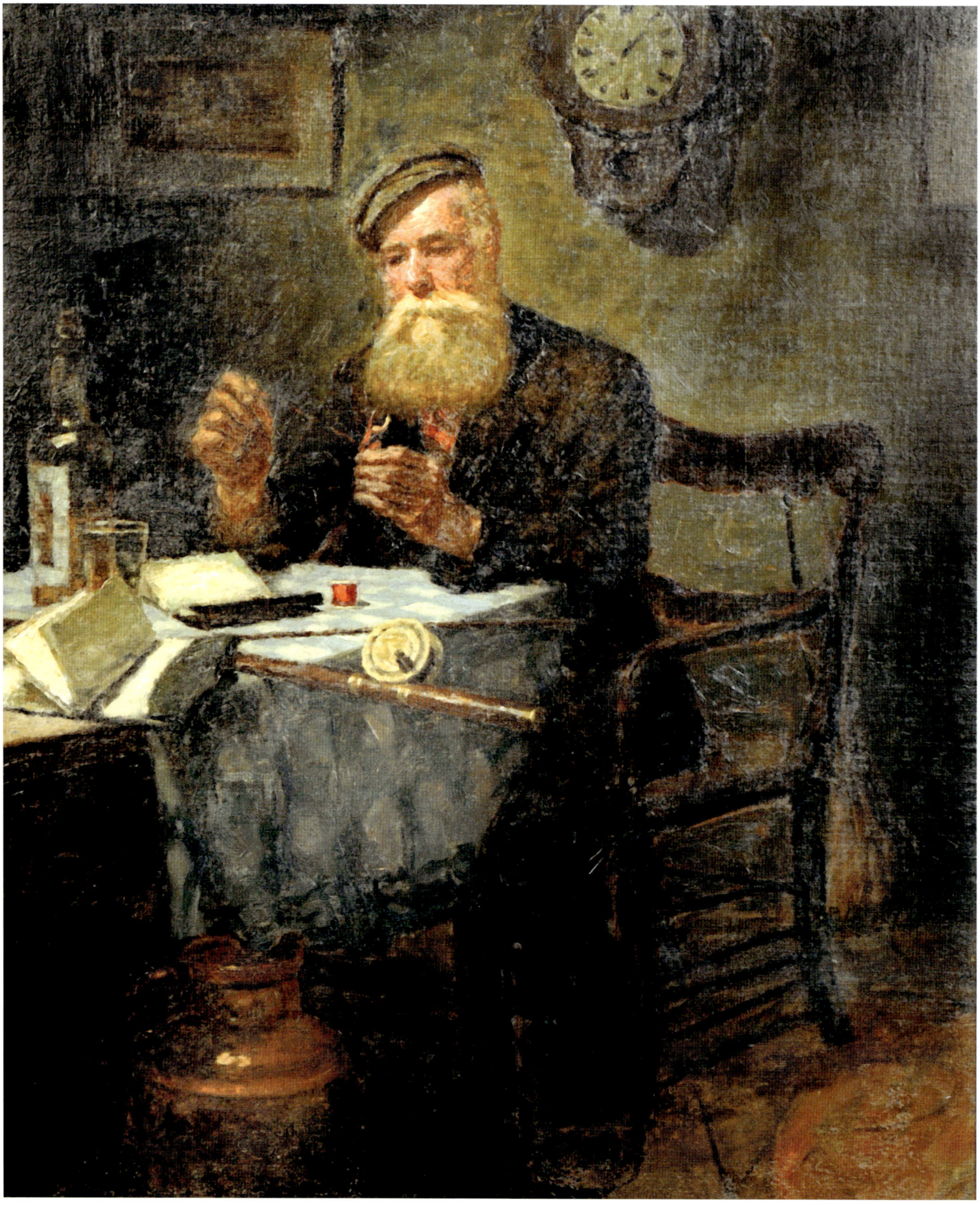

Dafi'r Felin as a Fisherman 1926 29" x 24"

6 TWILIGHT

When Carey was 84 years of age, he painted a portrait of his brother *Robert Morris* who was eight years his senior. Robert was an intelligent, distinguished-looking gentleman and Carey captured the essence of his personality in oils. Robert took a lively interest in Welsh and English literature and, like Carey, was a keen genealogist and a captivating raconteur. In his younger days he was a

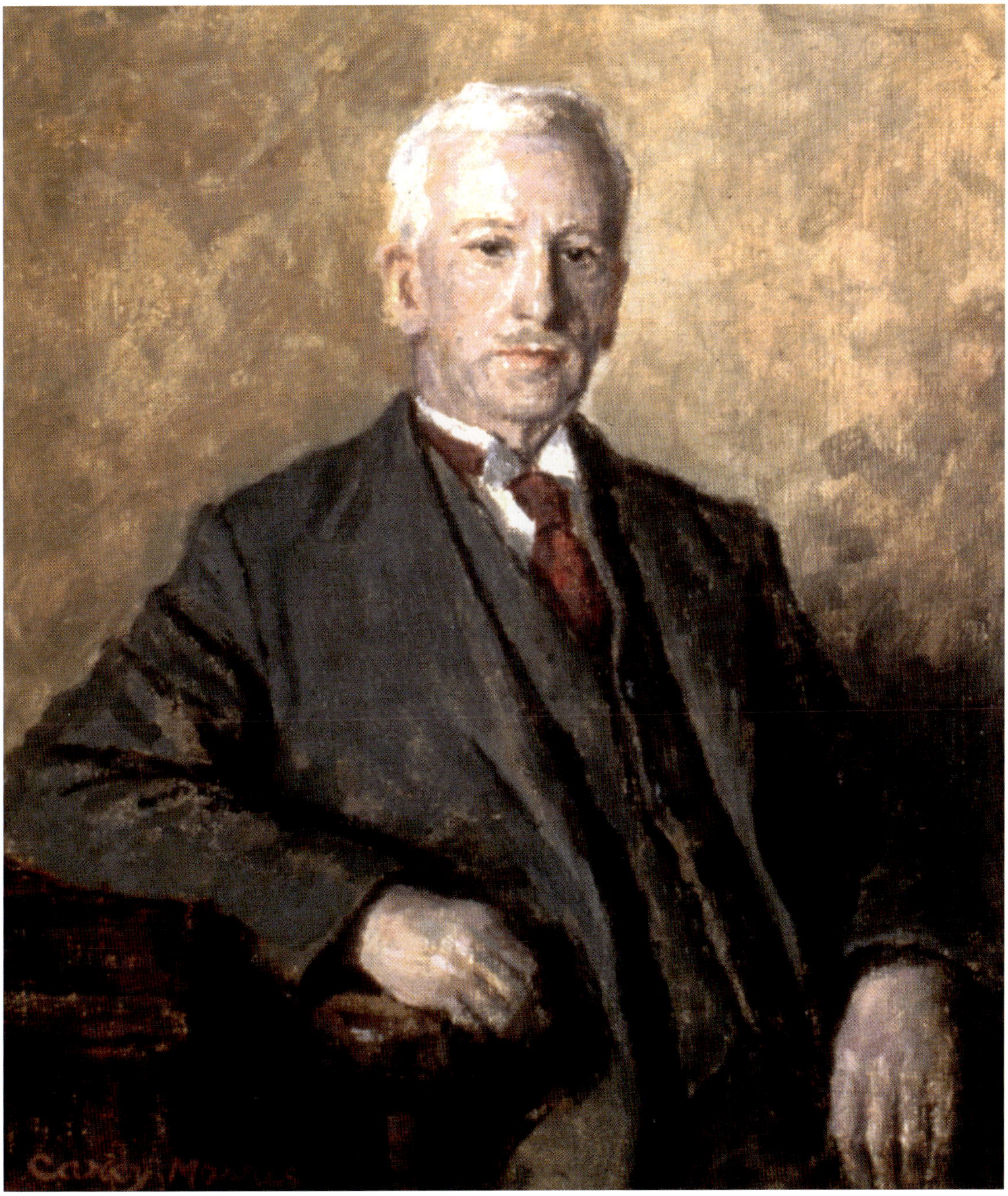

Robert Morris 1966 24" x 20"

well-known boulevardier. When he died aged 94, he was the last survivor of the most prestigious school in Llandeilo in those days, the Old Grammar School in Brynhyfryd House, Crescent Road which was near the present Dinefwr Council Offices. This school was superseded by the opening of Llandeilo County Intermediate, which later became the Grammar School in 1894.

Carey Morris exhibited at the Royal Academy of Arts in Piccadilly, the Royal Society of Portrait Painters in London; the Royal Glasgow Institute of the Fine Arts, the Royal Society of Artists in Birmingham and the London Salon. His works were also shown at the National Library of Wales, the Royal National Eisteddfod and at the Anglo-American Exhibition at White City, London as well as at exhibitions in Paris and Derby. He illustrated books, such as David Evans' translation into Welsh in 1929 of some of Hans Christian Andersen's *Fairy Tales* and Tegla Davies' translation into Welsh in 1931 of John Bunyan's *The Pilgrim's Progress*. He also illustrated children's books written by his wife.

Carey's training at the Newlyn School of Painting and the Slade School of Art enabled him to give expression to his innate artistry. He was born to be an artist, and his ability to make a character shine through his portraits remains uncanny. Carey always prided himself that he was able to make a living by painting, and he was one of the last of the artists who painted under the patronage of the squirearchy of Wales – many of these distinguished patrons became his friends.

As a true artist he felt sorry for those reduced to practicing abstract 'Art' and those who, in the late 1940s and early 1950s, performed freakish drip and splash abstract expressionism. These people laid

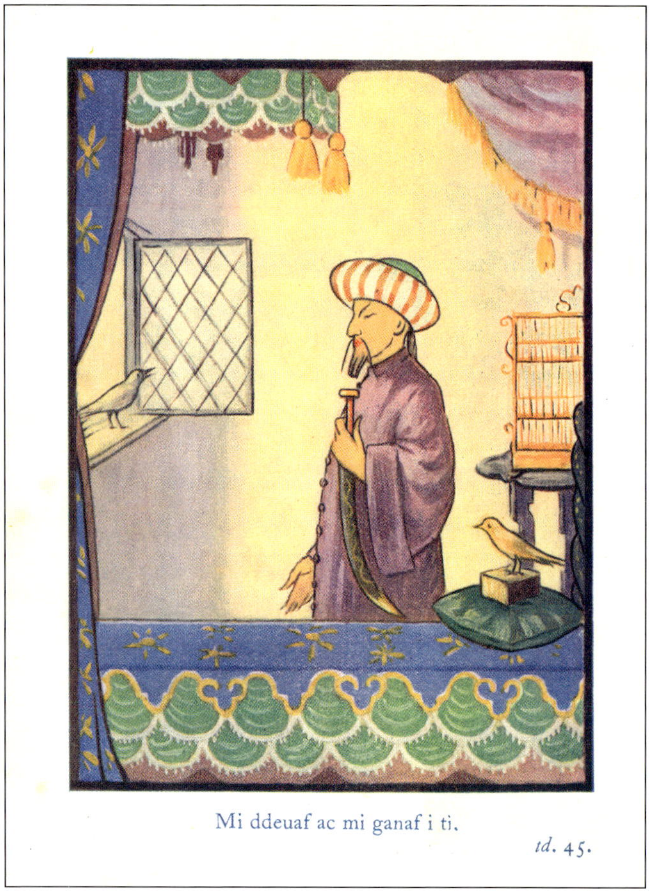

Yr Eos, Storïau Andersen / Andersen's Stories

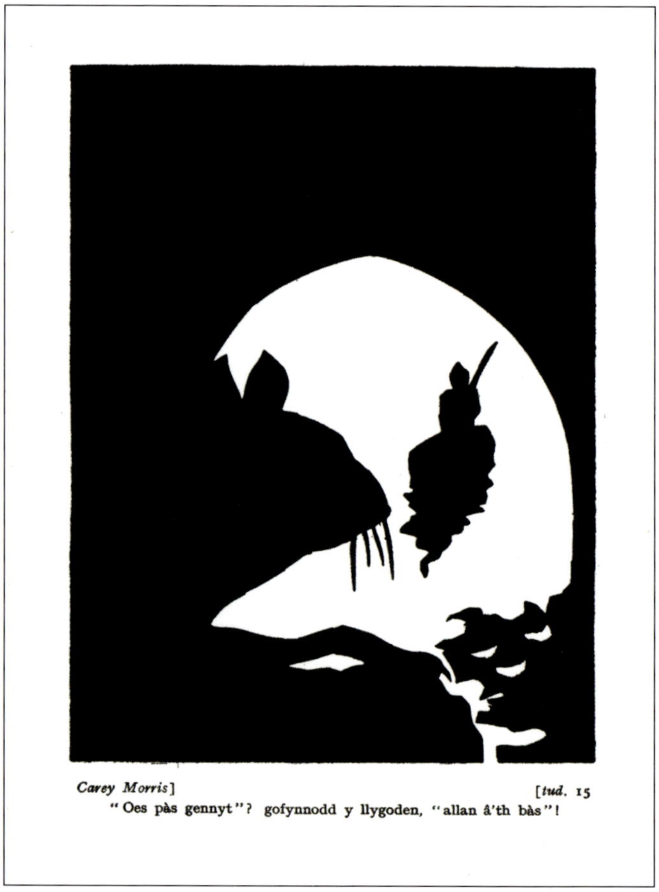

Y Milwr Tun, Storïau Andersen / Andersen's Stories

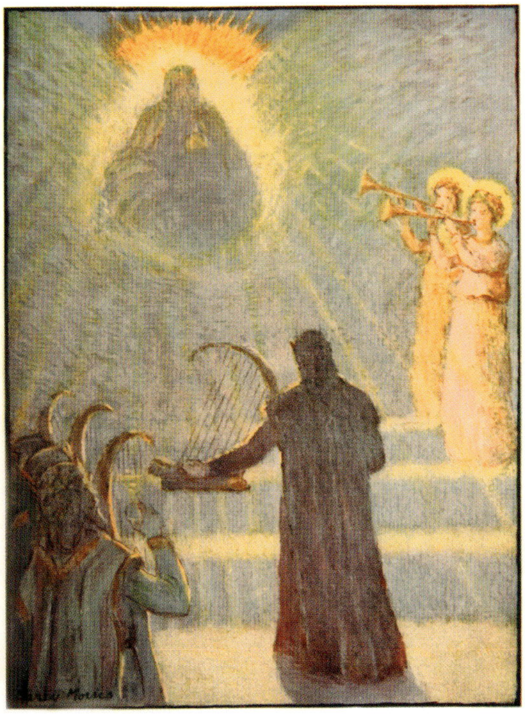

Tudalen 104

"Gerbron Un a eisteddai ar orsedd."

Breuddwyd Cristianna in John Bunyan's *Taith y Pererin / The Pilgrim's Progress*

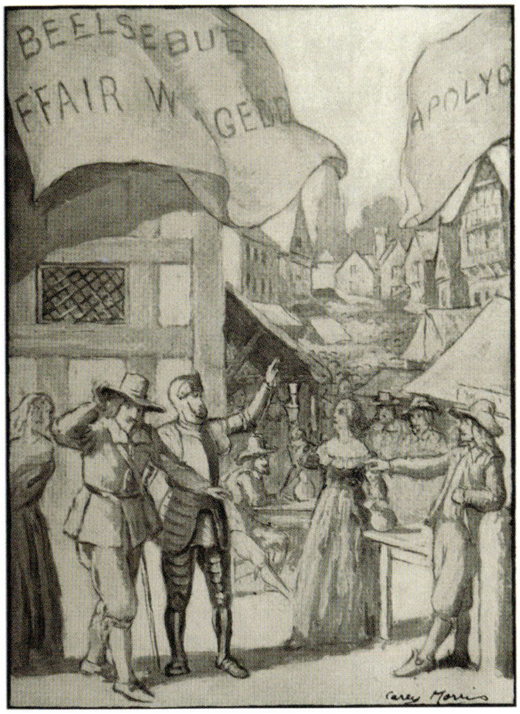

Tudalen 103.

" Rhythai'r bobl yn y ffair arnynt."

Ffair Wagedd in John Bunyan's *Taith y Pererin / The Pilgrim's Progress* 1931

canvases on the floor and, dancing in a frenzy, dripped paint from a can onto them – *Time* magazine called Jackson Pollock, its major proponent, 'Jack the Dripper'. However Pollock has now been challenged by the abstract conceptualist Tillanook Cheddar, who has so far had 20 solo exhibitions in five countries and has already sold 'art work' for £60,000. I can just see Carey roaring with laughter until he's blue in the face when he learns that this particular abstract conceptualist is a Jack Russell terrier, as reported in *The Times* of July 2009.

Andrew McNeillie, the poet and littérateur, was a friend of Carey Morris. He knew of Carey's belief that 'We have all been *had* by abstract painting', which Carey considered to be, 'A fad, a bid to be fashionable'. Referring to modern sculpture, Carey told Andrew McNeillie, 'When you see a couple of bedsteads stuck together, to me it's a lot of old ironmongery, which has its place, if it is to have one at all, in an engineering exhibition'. Carey told an amusing story about a man who had mistakenly commissioned a conceptual artist to paint a picture of the Israelites crossing the Red Sea. The finished picture consisted merely of a canvas covered in red paint. 'Where are the Israelites?' asked the man. 'They have just crossed,' said the 'artist'. Like those today who care, I can hear Carey proclaiming: '"Con-Art" – on a par with modern "Con-Verse"!' As long ago as 1935 Carey wrote, 'I have no use for any kind of art which tends towards "stunts". This kind of art has a short life and its success, if any, is ephemeral. Let us stand for pure art.'

In the black and white photograph of Carey's exquisite oil painting entitled *Dell*, his ability to reveal

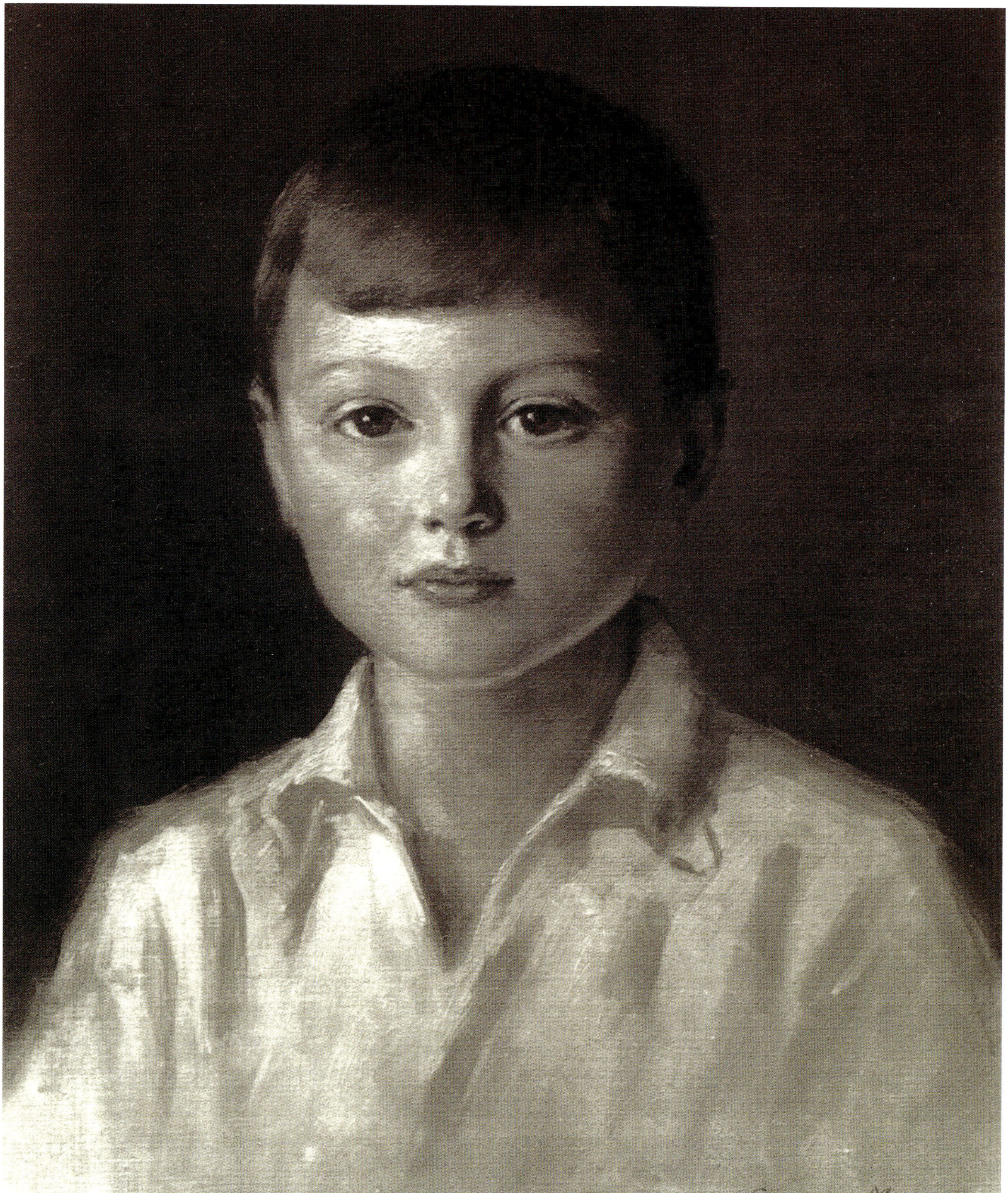

Dell *c.*1937 20" x 18"

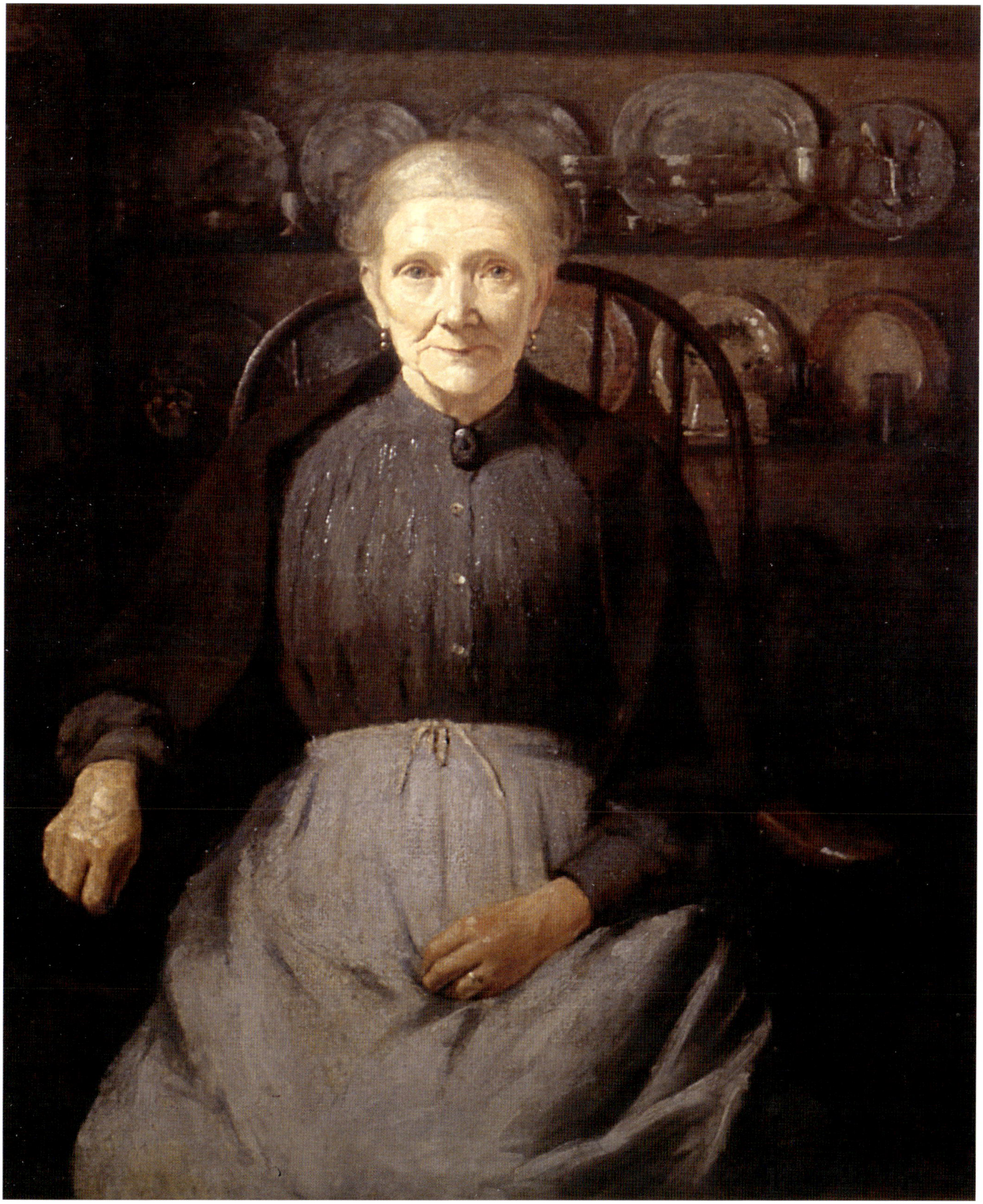

Lady and Seld 42" x 36½"

the innate nature of his subject becomes clear. It portrays the head of a young boy and captures, as far as it is possible, the innocence and ephemeral beauty of childhood. Unfortunately, the original oil painting itself could not be traced.

Carey's consummate skill in conveying to the viewer an impression of the personality of the subject in his portraits is evident in *Lady and Seld*. The placid old lady is sitting in her sack-back Windsor armchair in front of a pewter-laden 'seld' (Welsh dresser). This picture was probably painted in Ceredigion or Carmarthenshire. Her pale blue eyes look directly at the viewer and her thinning fair hair is drawn back, probably into a bun. Her gaze is steadfast and uncompromising, her forehead unlined and devoid of frown furrows. Her face is rather pale, in contrast to her hands which have a reddish tinge, suggesting she is not unused to manual work, and her apron remains in place. She is probably the wife or widow of a fairly prosperous farmer.

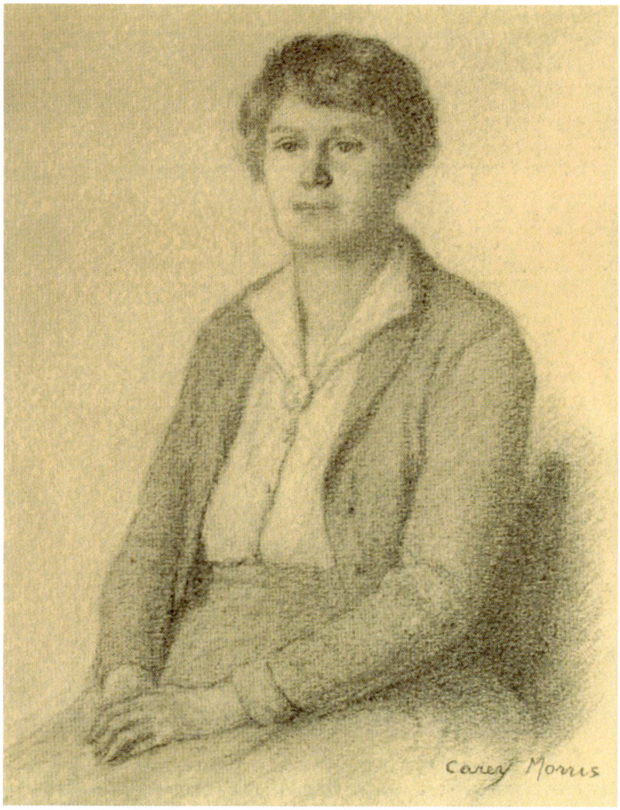

Eirwen Jones 11½" x 9"

His portraits of friends in the neighbourhood of Llandeilo are again striking examples of his ability to project personality visually. The far-seeing intellectual dedication to scholarship of author *Eirwen Jones* shines through his delicate pencil portrait of her. Carey's fine charcoal drawing of *The Pipe Smoker* depicts a man who regards the viewer attentively and with sympathetic concern. The strong hands of the late *Merfyn Williams* are those of a monumental mason, the left thumb hooked in his belt, the rakish tilt of his hat and quizzical expression, speak volumes about his colourful personality. But, perhaps the most telling portrayal of personality is to be seen in his charcoal drawing of *Gwynfor Evans* in 1951. Small wonder that this was the image chosen as a tribute to Gwynfor at the 2012 National Eisteddfod of Wales in the Vale of Glamorgan. The unflinching piercing contemplative look in the

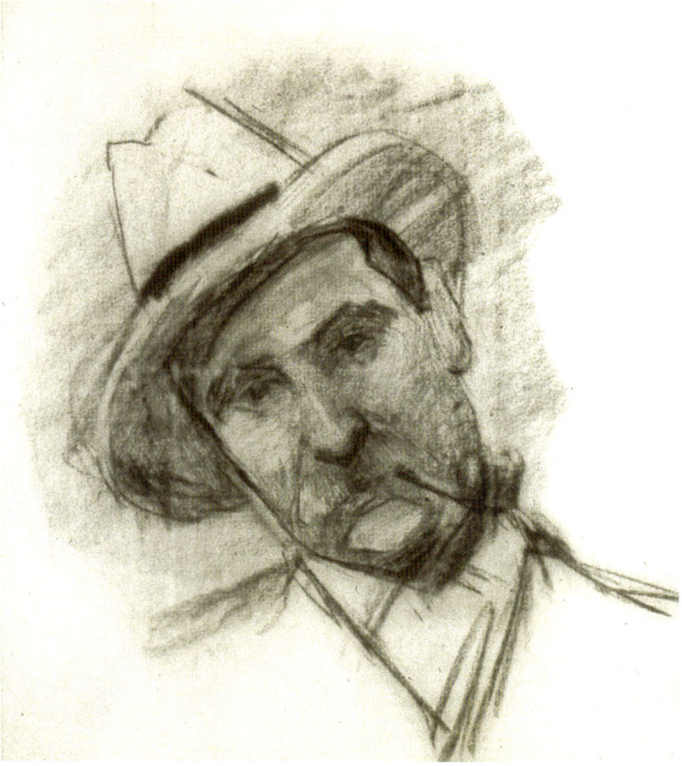

The Pipe Smoker 1905 17¾" x 15¼"

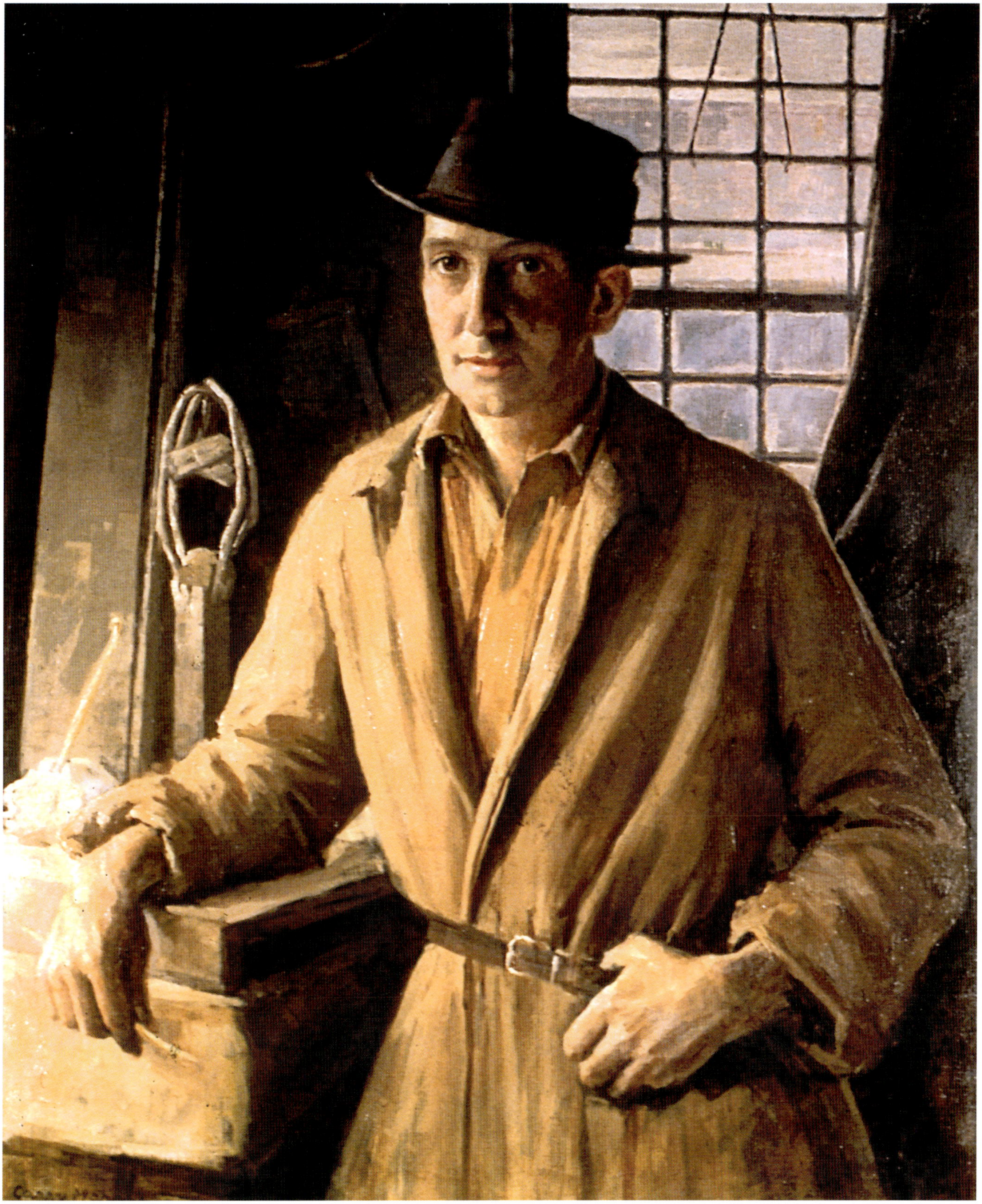

Merfyn Williams 36" x 29"

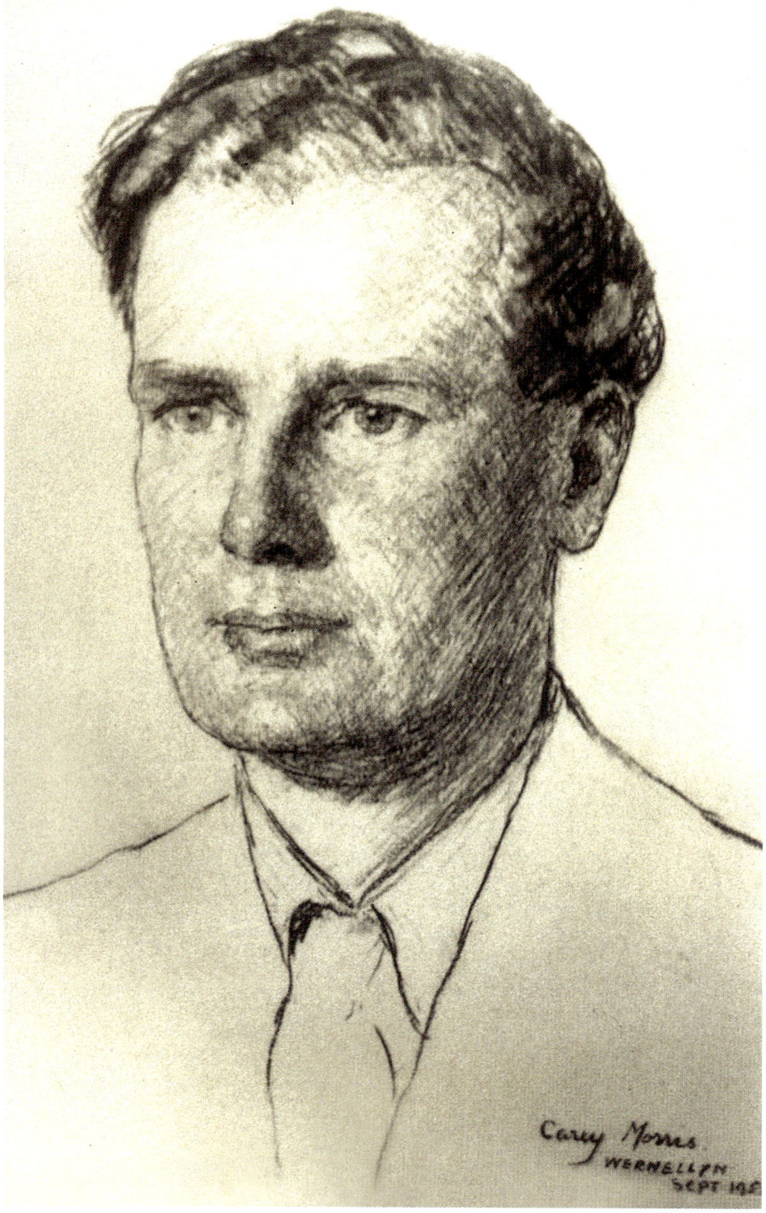

Gwynfor Evans 1951 15" x 11"

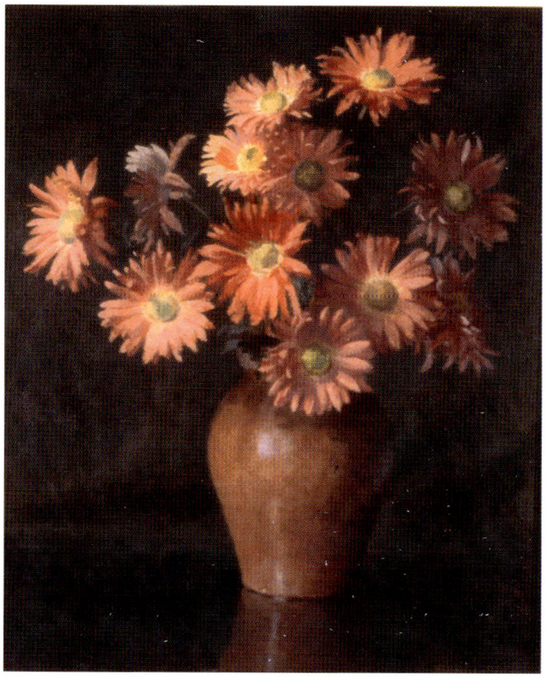

Dahlias 1930 22½" x 18"

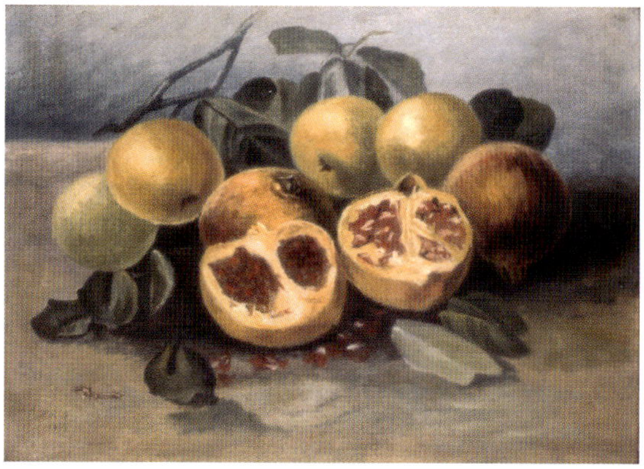

Pomegranates 1903

eyes focused on the far distant future with an expression of certainty, together with the determined set of the lips, are visual prophecies of the distinguished career of this future statesman.

Although primarily a portraitist, Carey has also given us images of still life. In his painting *Dahlias* the fresh, velvety, pleasing texture of the petals is vividly represented, as is the sturdy rustic glaze of the jug. The still-life *Pomegranates* again reveals Carey's ability to capture form, texture and tone in his paintings.

★ ★ ★ ★

Sometimes when I pass through Llandeilo now, late at night, I live again in my memory those happy times when there'd be a light in his window, and in answer to my tap, he'd open the door, and I would hear that strong cheerful voice of welcome, 'Croeso machgen i' [Welcome my boy]. I can still recall the inclined head, the extended arm offering his own fireside chair to his guest. Our storytelling and discussions on all manner of topics would last into the early hours of the morning, over innumerable mugs of what Carey called 'artists' tea', consisting of a handful of tealeaves from a caddy on the mantelpiece dropped into a mug of boiling water from the kettle on the hob, with a generous helping of very sweet condensed milk from a tin. Carey's interest in genealogy and his clear memory of events made him much sought after by local historians. His vivid 'word-pictures' of people he had known from all strata of society were painted on a canvas already illuminated by his personal experience of the true social conditions existing as far back as the last quarter of the nineteenth century.

Carey was a lovable person; he loved children, had a great sense of fun and shone in company, but unfortunately the promise of a brilliant artistic career, as evidenced by his pre-1914 work, was sadly blighted by World War I. Carey produced only one large Royal Academy painting after the war and, in fact, was largely forgotten. Since then, though he painted some superb portraits and landscapes, there were amongst them many obvious potboilers. That could well be due to the fact that his health was adversely affected after being a victim of gas inhalation during World War I. This rendered him, in his own words, 'a permanent semi-invalid', thus limiting the time he was able to concentrate continuously on his work during any one session. The frequent breaks he was obliged to take tended to destroy the smooth uninterrupted flow of work, essential to satisfy his own strict criteria for a successful painting. However, his courage and tenacity enabled him to continue to paint in spite of the ill-health for which he received a very small war pension.

He was a warm straightforward honest man, who was not afraid of saying what he meant as long as it was not hurtful to an individual. He was a nineteenth-century Christian gentleman, free from the Victorian vices. He had style. He was very fond of giving tea parties: I remember clearly the dining room with the distinctive wallpaper and a few of the portraits he had painted hanging in the room. After a portrait sitting he often gave a party, inviting a few friends. Carey and his brother Robert would sit at either end, with about six of us around the table – delicate old china and thin sandwiches – the conversation scintillating, Carey was a brilliant raconteur. He didn't suffer fools and had no time for poseurs – he had the ability to deflate them with a few well-chosen words.

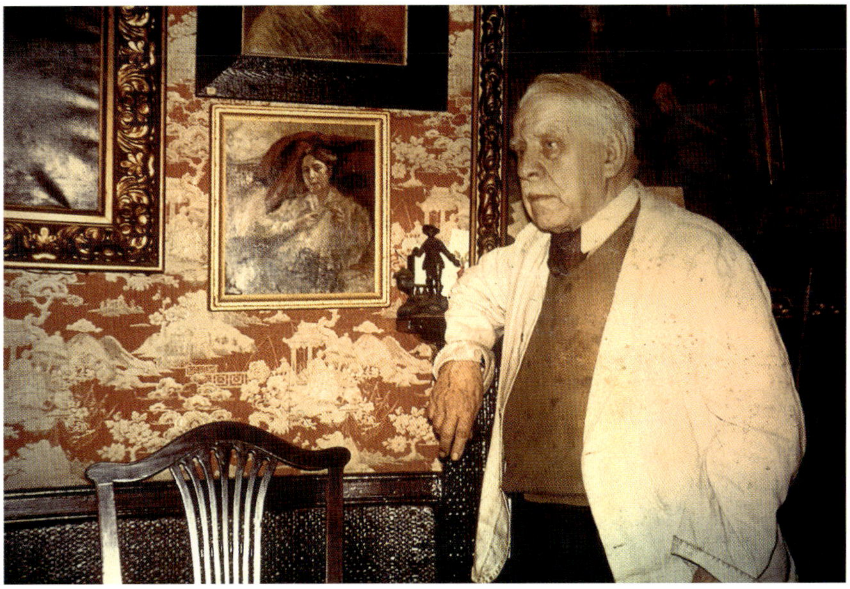

Carey in dining room

Many artists make and display self-portraits. One indication of Carey's freedom from ostentation lies in the fact that his only *self-portrait* did not come to light until after his death, and was found torn and folded in four under a pile of books. It required a great deal of expert attention to renovate it. The portrait, painted in the first decade of the twentieth century, shows Carey as a young man rather formally dressed holding brush and palette. Sir Kyffin Williams had this to say about Carey: "It is obvious to me that he has been neglected in Wales for he is obviously a very talented professional artist. It is certainly time to evaluate the work of Carey Morris.".

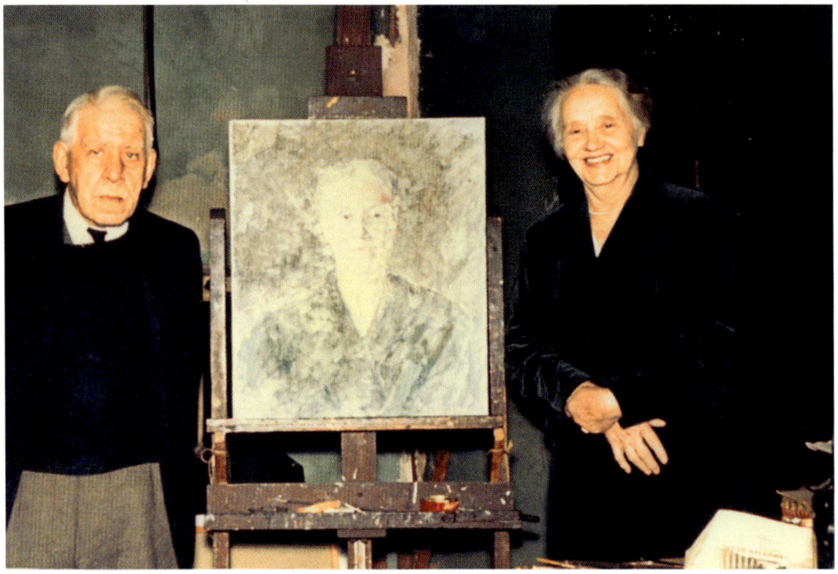

Sitter with a portrait in studio

Carey believed that empathy between artist and sitter, or artist and landscape, resulted in a picture containing many moods – something that cannot occur in a mere photograph. He pleaded for the Welsh Free Church to ditch Puritanism and embrace beauty in religion. He remembered travelling salesmen selling brightly coloured reproductions of the 'Madonna and Child', decorated with strips of glitter and gold and silver tinsel, to the country folk and thought it very amusing that travelling Jews were selling Roman Catholic pictures to Free churchgoers.

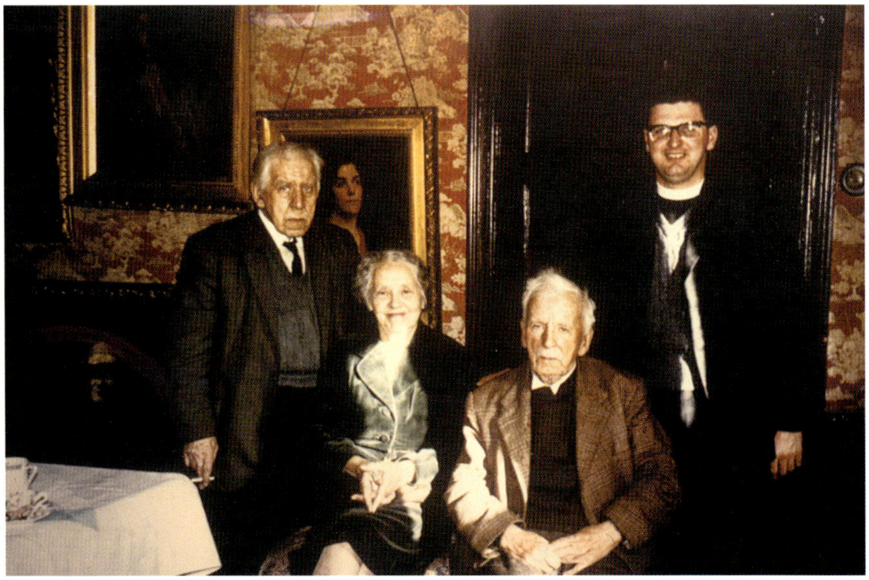

Carey's tea party

As a member of that dwindling society of professional artists, he was sympathetic to the efforts of gifted amateurs and gave them much guidance and encouragement. A professed appreciation of the arts opened the door of Carey Morris' house, and a true appreciation of traditional art led the way to his fireside.

Carey was painting right up to the day they took him into hospital. He died four days later, but his works are destined to shine through this century and beyond.

* * * *

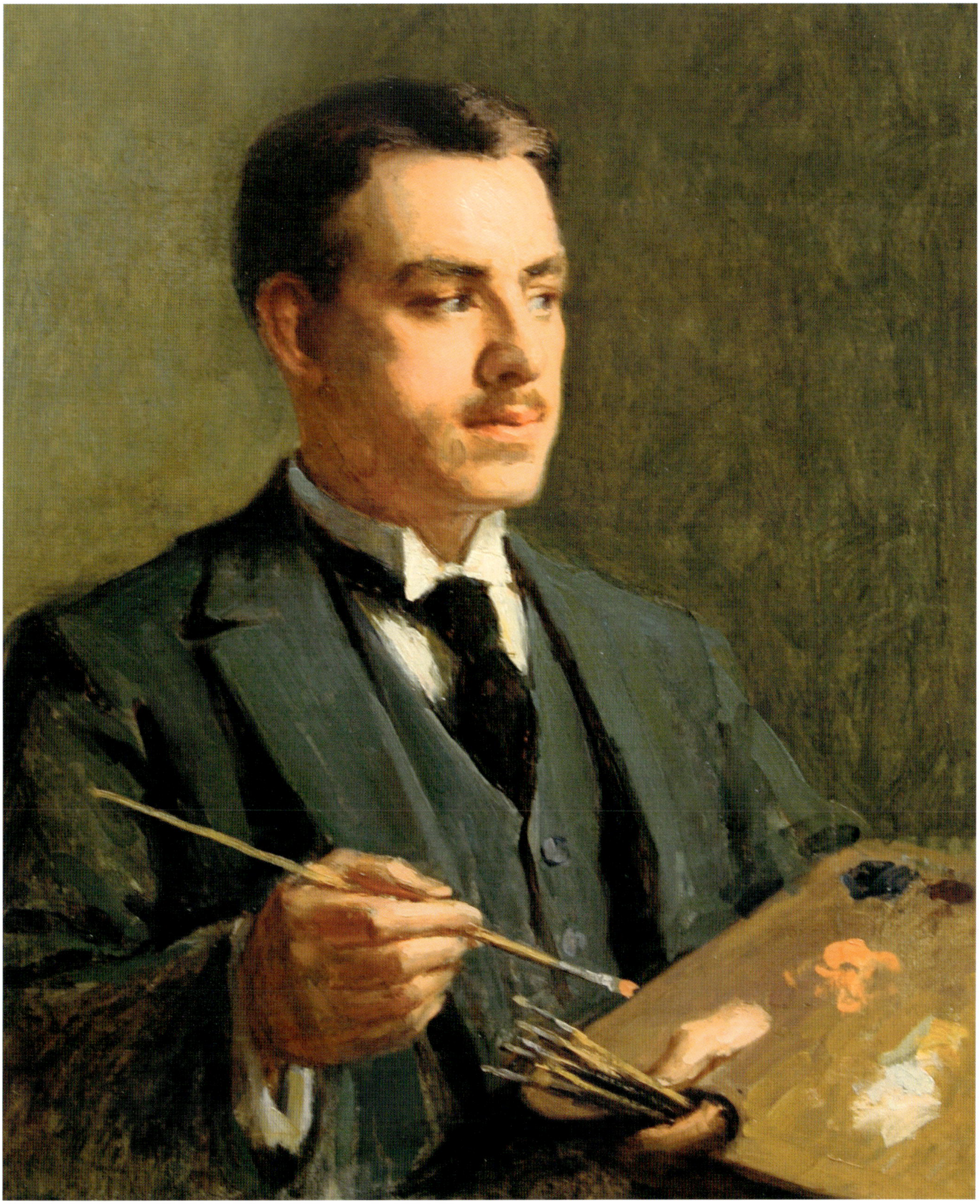

Carey's *Self-portrait* 1910 20" x 16"

Those who had the privilege of knowing Carey hold treasured memories of an unforgettable personality. That, which in any other context would be commonplace, became, in the company of Carey an occasion to remember and recall with pleasure. I have found that as the years pass, my memories of him have become even more precious. His knowledge of human nature was profound, and his selflessness was touching in its simplicity. His constant concern for the spiritual and physical well-being of his fellow man was evident even up to the very last moments of his life. He died, as he had lived, with natural dignity.

Those of us who were present at his graveside on that grey November day cannot forget the eerie occurrence as his coffin was lowered into the grave. After his burial that day, we walked back to his deserted studio, and there on his easel was his last portrait, *Ann* – unfinished – the paint scarcely dry.

Gŵr mwyn oedd Carey, yn hael ei gymwynas,
Rhoddodd gyfoeth ein cenedl, yn gof ar gynfas.

His strokes of genius, our lost memory,
Now visual treasure, thanks to Carey.

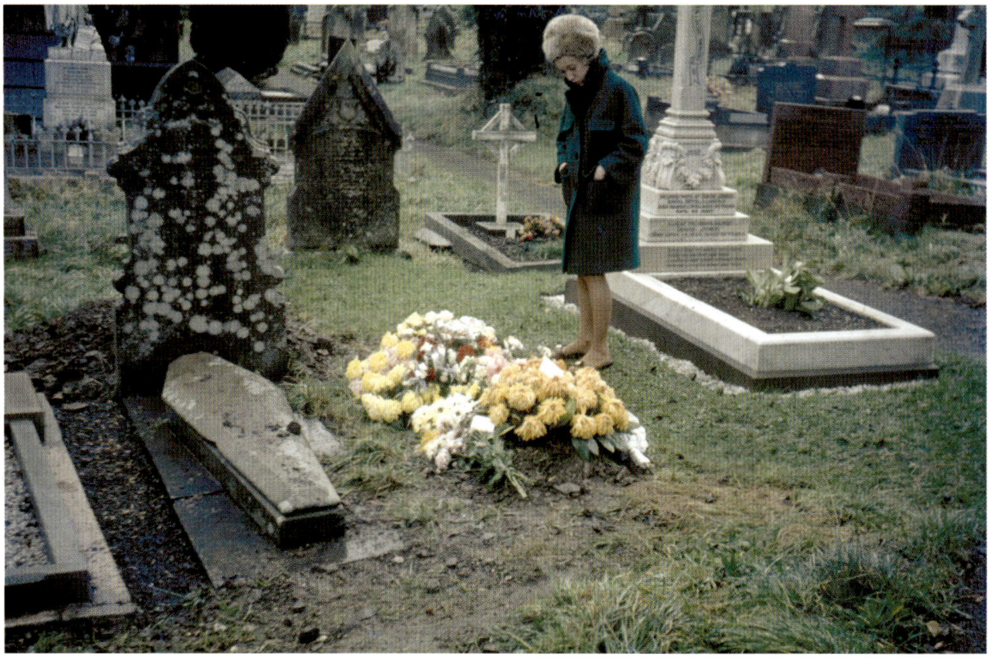

Carey's grave

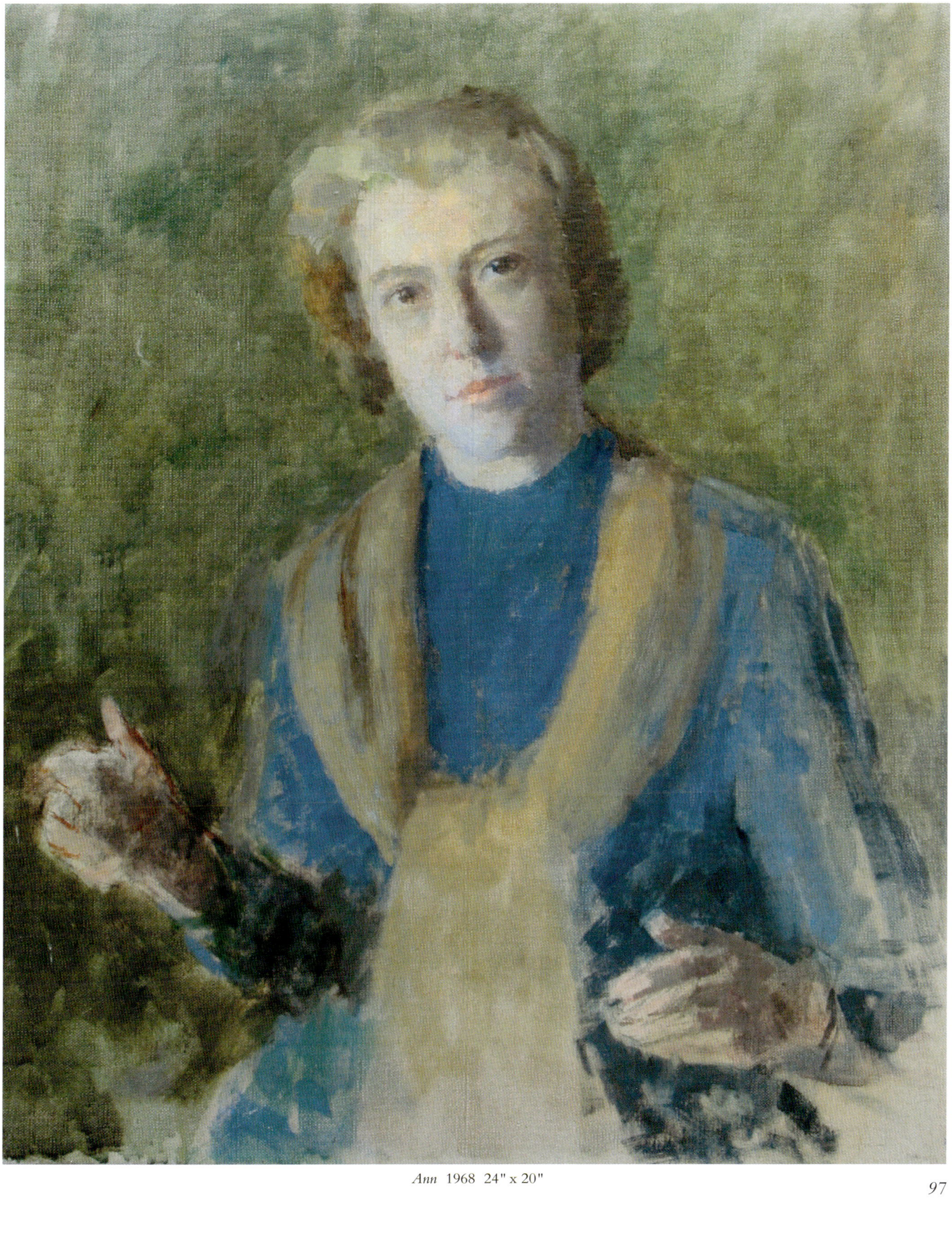

Ann 1968 24" x 20"

APPENDIX I

Welsh Weavers

Though not visible, there is another source of light coming from outside the picture on the right-hand side, illuminating the winding wheel and casting its shadow on to the window wall. To the left side of the old lady is the skein-winder (sometimes called a 'swift' or 'wool-servant') and the undyed wool, wound around its four upright adjustable pegs, appears to be flooded with light from both sources, as does the blue, red and beige wool on the weft-bobbins. The plants in the earthenware pot and blue bowl on the windowsill are also well-lit by both light sources. In contrast, the wicker basket which holds the weft-bobbins and the skein of wool spilling over the edge of the basket, as well as the three-legged milking stool, are in shadow.

The rust coloured bricks which stabilise the platform at the base of the stout leg, around which the skein-winder rotates, although in deep shadow, can nevertheless be recognised. The winding wheel shown has no pedals and is hand operated. It is a smaller edition of the Great Wheel and would be very much cheaper to buy than a spinning wheel. Mrs Edwards is turning the winding wheel with her right hand on the rim instead of using the handle shown on the horizontal spoke just below her right forearm. The drive cord on the winding wheel and the peg holes in the wooden arms of the skein-winder are very clearly shown, as is the thread being fed on to it to be coiled into a skein or hank. The four skein-winder pegs are adjustable giving different sized skeins of wool.

Carey Morris shows the same meticulous attention to detail in his depiction of the flying-shuttle handloom seen in the background of the picture. Mr Edwards is shown wearing a leather wrist-strap, using his right hand to pull the flying-shuttle to his left, in order to weave the weft thread between the warp threads. His left hand, hidden by the top of the shaft, is on the cloth-beater (also out of view) which beats the thread into the cloth. The wool on the warp beam is immediately obvious, but almost occludes the cloth beam carrying the finished material. Even the cord heddles, each having an eye through which a warp thread can be passed, are visible, descending from the shaft which is seen above the warp beam. At the left end of the warp beam, but barely visible, are the three boxes housing the three flying-shuttles, each carrying a different coloured thread resulting in a tricoloured finished material. Against a light brown back wall, three of the pulleys that operate the heddle-shafts are clearly visible, while the fourth pulley can be seen in front of Mr Edwards' left arm. At the base of the loom the pedal cords and shafts are distinctly seen.

APPENDIX II

In 1982 Lynn Hughes organized a very successful exhibition of Carey Morris' work which I was honoured to open. Following this, the Carey Morris Centenary Committee and Llandeilo Town Council placed a commemorative plaque on Carey's house.

Carey Morris' easel is still in occasional use by the young talented artist, Joseph Galvin, winner of the 2008 prestigious award given annually by the Royal Society of Portrait Painters. He has painted the easel as it is today. Carey would have been delighted to have known this.

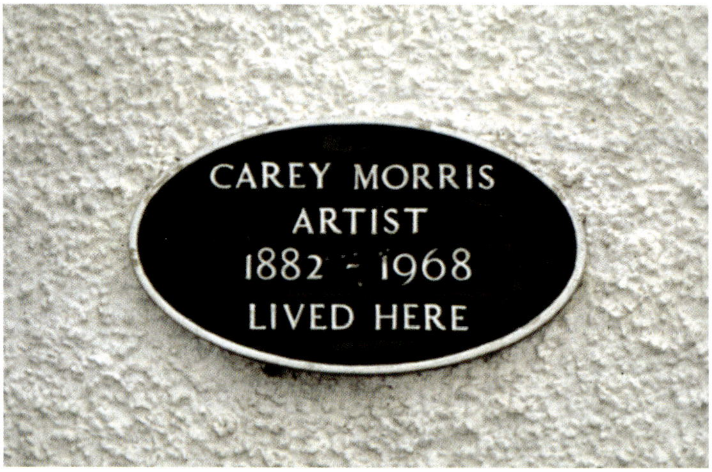

The plaque on Carey's house

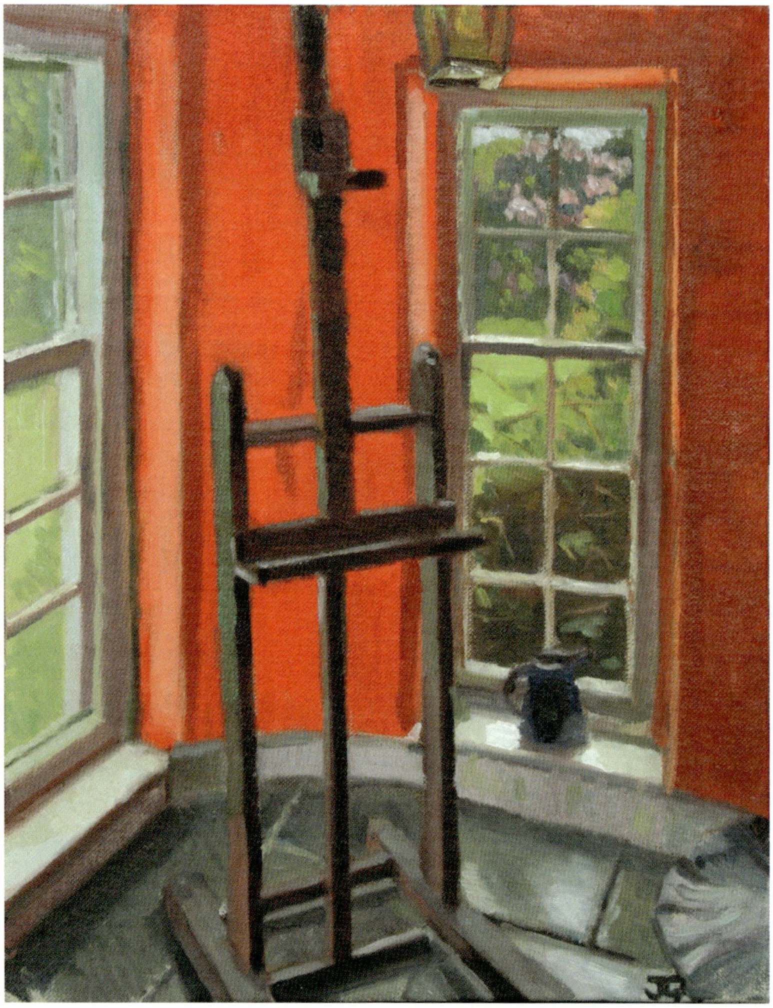

Carey's Empty Easel 2012 15" x 10"

BIBLIOGRAPHY

Chilvers, Ian and Osbourne, Harold and Farr, Dennis, *The Oxford Dictionary of Art*, Oxford, 1997.

Crystal, David, *The Cambridge Biographical Encyclopaedia,* Cambridge, 1995.

Fox, Caroline, *Stanhope Forbes and the Newlyn School,* Newton Abbot, 1993.

Fraser, Maxwell, *Introducing West Wales*, 1956.

Goscombe-John, Sir William, *Transactions of the Honourable Society of Cymmrodorion,* London, 1924.

Green, Iris, *Posing the Model*, Penzance, 2002.

Greenlaw, Joanna, *Swansea Clocks (including Llanelli, Llandeilo and Neath)*, Llandybïe, 1997.

Gruffydd, W.T., *Hanes y Tabernacl Llandeilo*, Llandysul, 1951.

Inglis-Jones, Elisabeth, *Peacocks in Paradise*, 1950.

Jones, Eirwen, *The Carmarthenshire Historian*, 1978.

Langley, Roger, *Walter Langley, Pioneer of the Newlyn Art Colony,* Bristol, 1997.

Lloyd, Thomas, *The Lost Houses of Wales*, 1989.

Lloyd, Thomas, *Gower*, 1989.

Lord, Peter, *Y Chwaer-Dduwies: Celf, Crefft a'r Eisteddfod*, Llandysul, 1992.

Lord, Peter, *The Visual Culture of Wales: Industrial Society*, Cardiff, 1998.

Lord, Peter, *Winifred Coombe Tennant: A Life through Art*, Aberystwyth, 2007.

McNeillie, Andrew, *Slower*, 2006.

Miles, Dillwyn, *The Royal National Eisteddfod of Wales*, Swansea, 1978.

Miles, Dillwyn, *The Secrets of the Bards of the Isle of Britain*, Llandybïe, 1992.

Morris, Carey, *Transactions of the Honourable Society of Cymmrodorion*, London, 1924.

Morris, Carey, Personal communications.

Owen, Wilfred, *Mapping Golgotha*, Gregynog, 2007.

Peate, Iorwerth, *Clock and Watchmakers in Wales*, Llandysul, 1945 and 1960.

Phillips, Bethan, *Peterwell*, Llandysul, 1983.

Phillips, Bethan, *Dihirod Dyfed*, Wrecsam, 1991.

Rhys, Glyn, *Yr Enfys, Wales International*, Llandysul, 2001.

Rhys, Glyn, *Fflam Dwy Ganrif*, Llandysul, 2002.

Rhys, Glyn, *The Carmarthenshire Antiquary*, Llandybïe, 2008.

Roberts, R.G., *Cofiant y Parchedig Williams Davies, Llandeilo*, 1975.

Stephens, Meic (ed.), *The Oxford Companion to the Literature of Wales*, Oxford, 1986.

Thomas, Sir Daniel Lleufer, *Transactions of the Honourable Society of Cymmrodorion*, London, 1924.

Thomas, Edward, *The Poems of John Dyer*, London, 1903.

Wheeler, Sir Mortimer, *Transactions of the Honourable Society of Cymmrodorion*, London, 1924.

Williams-Ellis, Sir Clough, *Transactions of the Honourable Society of Cymmrodorion*, London, 1924.

Williams, Isaac, *Transactions of the Honourable Society of Cymmrodorion*, London, 1924.

Williams, Sir Kyffin, Personal Communications.

INDEX

M

N

O

P

PICTURE INDEX